WILLIAM CUMMINGS
TEL.: (47) 22 36 22 16

1989

TO BE KEPT IN TACT

GUIDE BOOK

Monday Feb 19, 1990 7:00 ...

You cant emagine the lonelyness that I am feeling right now. I have sat here by myself all day long. I have gone through my address book 3 or 4 time looking at each of the names in it and finding no one that I would like to spend my day with but one person. But I cant be with this person.

Monday Feb 19, 1990 6:00 PM Brono's Restaurant
Tuesday Feb 20, 1990 9:00 AM Rockefeller suply Room

I have my heath and that is one of the biggest blessing of life. Do not be affraid to go through life. Have it be a fantastic adventure.

HOW WOULD I LIVE MY LIFE IF I THOUGHT I HAD ONLY 10 YEARS LEFT.

1. I would be much braver in persuing Artistic objectives
   a) create with out the concern of the market place
2. My convictions about what I believe would be stronger.
3. I would ask for help to get what I want
4. I would have a "go for it" mentality
5. I would work to share my soul with another person 4/15/90
6. I would love someone only for the sake of love 5/5/90
7. I would do bigg and exciting things 6/8/90

White Light

Heiberg Cummings Design

PHOTOGRAPHY
Keith Scott Morton

ESSAYS
Kjersti Sundt Sissener
Øivind Storm Bjerke
Svein Olav Hoff
William Cummings

THE MONACELLI PRESS

KODAK TMY 5053
STOP
STOP

The collaboration between Bernt Heiberg and Bill Cummings goes back to the day they met on a street in Warsaw in 1990. They have since created a partnership in their life and work where they complement and inspire each other. Heiberg Cummings Design has established offices in Oslo and New York. Commissions include public offices, restaurants, and private houses. The geographical distribution spans Europe and the United States, from Norway to France to Martha's Vineyard and Long Island; from rugged high mountains to the top of a skyscraper; from the hip Hamptons to sun-drenched, tropical Key Biscayne. The clients are equally diverse, of varying backgrounds and in all stages of life. Bernt and Bill value their close relationship with all their clients. The projects vary from small apartments to large manors, from cabins to estates to equestrian farms. The types of home vary, as do the landscapes and environments in which the homes find themselves. But there is a recurring theme: in all the projects Heiberg Cummings creates a concept and subsequently develops an individualized design in close collaboration with the client.

Purity of Creative Thought –

Do not discard your personal sucess for the pursuit of anothers Idea of sucess. Success is different for all People and each persons nation of sucess is as valid as the next person's.

Go to your book and study your principles of life and make sure that the people very close to you understand it and respect it.

Your truth has been revealed to you. Now you must study it and internalize it so that you may apply it to practical day to day living.

You will continue to discover new facits of life, but always bare in mind your ==original thought.==

CARTE POSTALE

you
(a beat) We are
who you are. (a beat)
angry,
can't stay together
I'm who I am ... and you
fuck yourself, Shephard.

Heiberg Cummings Design's New York office is in Chelsea, an area filled with prominent American and international galleries. In the early 1990s, many former commercial and industrial buildings in the neighborhood stood empty. When rents in Soho went up, a number of galleries moved to Chelsea, making the district a vibrant cultural center where visitors can go from one exhibition to the next, from one innovative mode of artistic expression to the next. The High Line, a former railway line, been transformed into an exciting park with grass and wildflowers growing between idle railway tracks. Thousands of people visit the High Line every week, and Bill Cummings is one of them. When Bill goes to work, he likes to take a route along the High Line. Perhaps listening to an audio book on theoretical physics, he studies plants, observes birds, and thinks about the dreams and flights of fancy of his clients. On the other hand, Bernt Heiberg and his dog Flink like to walk to the office along Tenth Avenue—they have many places to stop to exchange greetings and many people waiting for a daily hug. You look beautiful today, have a wonderful day, Bernt says and smiles. Flink offers an extra hug.

Heiberg Cummings saw the potential of Chelsea years ago and bought offices in a former industrial building that was going to be converted into housing units. There is always a buzz of dynamic activity about the office. Clients and consultants come and go. The telephone rings continuously. Bernt and Bill hurry off to meetings and site visits. Flink has a fixed position on a chair next to Katie White, the indispensable "air traffic controller" who keeps tabs on all the appointments and assignments. Quite a few gatherings are held on the office premises, and exhibitions are organized with Norwegian and American artists.

Material Wholeness: An Intellectual Concept

The interior design projects shown in this book represent a broad spectrum, but a limited selection, of the commissions Heiberg Cummings Design has carried out over more than twenty years. The works show the designers' spatial solutions and also their choice of colors, furniture, and textiles. In certain cases, Heiberg Cummings has designed the building as well as the interior; in others, the designers have altered the plan of the rooms within a given framework: walls have been moved, kitchen areas redefined, bathrooms completely rehabilitated, staircases built, or windows changed. It is clear that designing a home means something more far-reaching than making sure the cushions match.

All the objects in an interior have to support the overall principle. Each room can be defined as an installation consisting of individual elements that are interrelated: furniture, objects, fabrics, materials, and colors. Each element is part of a whole and has a relation to all the other elements in the space. One of the distinctive characteristics of Heiberg Cummings Design is that the wholes are so thoroughly thought through that the number of elements can be reduced without losing the feeling of a totality: if objects are removed one by one—a cushion here, a chair there, a table—the overall impression will not disappear, even when just one or two objects remain, such as a carpet and a sofa. The same is true if the objects are reinstated in parallel fashion. A client could put it like this: "Bernt and Bill will make a plan for my living room with curtains, sofas, cushions, tables, and carpets. I have to spread out the investment and buy just a few things at a time. But I know that even if I start with just a sofa and a curtain, everything will ultimately come together. It is up to me to decide when all the pieces will be in place."

The assignments carried out by Heiberg Cummings Design are characterized by a conscious blend of straight lines, round shapes, patterns, and unexpected elements. A defined dynamic in the differences between the elements of the interior is a recurrent theme. This dynamic creates the tension and harmony that are felt when a visitor enters a room. In an interior, a sofa might have a high and straight back with equally high and straight side panels. The owner might slip into the stringent construction and become enclosed, as if in a soft nest. A large, round lamp base of transparent glass dominates a small, fragile square table. Light streams in through curtains of light linen, falling onto a soft cushion that has been plumped and positioned with utmost precision. A rectangular table has leaf-shaped legs, a square table spiral legs. Straight, black sash bars of iron form rectangular panes in a wall of glass that divides a room into two sections. Bedsteads are often high, with vertical rectangular panels. Oblong, horizontal tiles are laid over each other in broken columns. Surfaces on tables, benches, and backs of chairs are often worn, the paint peels, the life of an object is reflected in its surface. Stains and stripes are welcome. "The objects are allowed to live a life that is parallel to the life of the owners," Bernt Heiberg says. "I am happy when I see glass marks or scratches in a tabletop. Then I can see that the dining table has been used and that it represents a place where people have enjoyed being together."

The textiles Heiberg Cummings uses have a clearly defined texture and structure. Velvet can be soft and caressing, linen hard and ruckled. It is in their combination that the essence and the distinctive nature of each textile become evident. A striped armchair can have one cushion in a different color and another made from old rice sacks. The patterns may merge or highlight each other. Contrasts and subdued transitions are also reflected in the choice of colors. The nuances of one complement and challenge those of another. Each bit of color, each piece of a pattern, and every texture are carefully chosen. An unexpected color choice or a shape that seemingly does not belong creates power and tension in an interior. The unexpected element might be a pair of rococo candlesticks on a modern table or a baroque dresser with a contemporary mirror above it. Perhaps it is a worn orange corner of a carpet under a dining table. Or it can be the red interior of a kitchen cupboard. Form and texture, along with color, might provide the unexpected element. It is often this unanticipated component that supports the concept for the interior design project—the unexpected reinforces the overall aim of the designers. Straight lines, soft shapes, an awareness of the tactile values of materials, a sensitivity to color, and a bit of a surprise reveal the overall aim for the space defined by the designers and requested by the owner.

This overall aim, the idea of the function of the interior for its owner, the concept of the installation, is the most important dimension for Bill Cummings and Bernt Heiberg. To create an interior that involves a concrete manifestation of longings and fantasies is a principal goal. The concepts underlying Heiberg Cummings commissions are abstract—it can be something as apparently simple as "cozy." Or it may be as specific as the owner's dream of a harmonious family life in the mountains in deserted countryside, where squalls of wind are the only uncontrolled change of mood. For a client who has lost a partner and wants to create a life as a single person, the concept can have to do with being happy about being on one's own. Perhaps instead it is an owner who has just fallen in love and wants to set up a home with the attachment between the couple as its focus. The owner may have dreams—perhaps he or she is looking for a place where personal boundaries may be transcended. To try out the unknown, to give the chance of renewing ingrained habits: these are examples of concepts that can be given form with the help of interior design. To live in a particular way in relation to a building, town, or neighborhood is another angle of approach for determining the concept. It is these abstract concepts that Heiberg Cummings Design seeks to define and subsequently realize through design.

Facing page, from top: Designers William Cummings and Bernt Heiberg, with their Jack Russell terrier, Flink, at home in Manhattan. Nineteenth-century Scandinavian portraits on an antique Norwegian chest. This page: The Chippendale-inspired settee is 19th-century Norwegian. See Resources.

cool and cozy

New York designing duo Bernt Heiberg and William Cummings import the magic of Norway to a tidy Chelsea duplex

Text by Mark Welsh · Photography by William Waldron · Produced by Elizabeth Sverbeyeff Byron

Break out the aquavit if a Norwegian should ever call your home *koselig.* Literally translated, it means cozy, and in Norway the word is used to describe everything from a room's hospitable warmth to the pleasant feeling one gets upon running into an old friend. For Norwegian-born Bernt Heiberg, the duplex he shares with William Cummings in Manhattan's Chelsea neighborhood is about as *koselig* as things get. For starters, it's small.

"We've lived in much bigger houses, but we didn't use half the rooms," says Heiberg. "Size doesn't matter that much to us. And the scale of this place makes it feel like home."

When the two met a dozen years ago, Heiberg had an antiques shop in Oslo, and Cummings, a Colorado native, was working in Europe as an interiors photographer. They bonded over a mutual love of primitive painted chairs and Swedish meatballs, and in 1990 opened Heiberg Cummings Design in Oslo. The reviews were hushed. "Back then people in Norway didn't really work with designers," Heiberg recalls. "They'd be embarrassed and say, 'Please don't tell anyone we used you.'"

These days, with an outpost in New York and an international clientele clamoring for the pair's celebrated "neo-Scandinavian" style, people are far more likely to implore them "to please tell everyone we used you." Known for mixing modern ideas with historical Nordic

KELLY HOPPEN

"Uncle Bernt, Uncle Bernt"—the greeting accompanies a pattering of small feet over the flooring planks—"thank you so much, you've made my room as beautiful as that of a princess," the flaxen-haired slip of a girl in school uniform calls out, throwing herself into his arms. Inside the dining room her little sister jumps up and down, up and down, on the new sofa in honor of the visitors. Professional black-and-white photographs of the children and the family cover many of the walls. From the hall comes the sound of practicing on the grand piano, one and two and three, one and two and three. This is a home that centers on family life and shared experiences. Father's deep bass voice and happy laughter boom through the rooms. Mother adroitly balances tasks: she talks, smiles, picks up the phone, and makes sandwiches while planning who is going to drive the kids to lacrosse, football, and tennis—and all the while she is busy wrapping a birthday present in beautiful paper with a large silk bow. "We had a lot of fun together, doing this project," Bernt and Bill say, sharing a hug with their elegant hostess. "And I love every detail that they came up with," she replies. The project is a newly built house on the East Coast, inspired by French architecture, that conveys the impression it has always been there. An austere facade with large, iron-framed windows affords a fine view over the sea; a lawn disappears over the horizon; large flowering trees take the breath away; a swimming pool steals around the corner of the house. Inside, the large kitchen is the natural hub of family activities. And now the family has acquired a sweet little black curly-coated puppy. A bundle of joy, they all agree.

American Houses
Words That Matter
Colonial Revival House

YAMAHA

KODAK
46
5

to accept the things
I cannot change
Courage to change
the things I can
and Wisdom
to know the
difference.
TOCCA
Cleopatra
HERMES
PARIS

ST. TROPEZ

KODAK 4
KODAK
46
KODAK 400TX

256
800-TO-899
256
DOOR
900-TO-999

D
R KNOB
OUND
NOBS

Bill Cummings and Bernt Heiberg cross a worn threshold to enter the premises of the brasswork shop P. E. Guerin. Here brass is shaped by hand according to nineteenth-century patterns. The narrow four-story house in New York's Greenwich Village shelters a showroom, a foundry, and a factory dating from 1892. An enormous brown cat has fallen asleep on a heap of old pattern drawings. Drawers in a complex conglomeration are labeled as servant bells, clock balls, spear heads, hinges, and so on. The drawers cover high walls in an elongated, closely furnished showroom with a vast number of small objects made of bronze and brass. The founder of the company, Pierre Emmanuel Guerin, emigrated from Brittany to New York in 1857. With him he brought large crates of old patterns and molds from his brass-molding firm.

The present-day proprietor, Andrew F. Ward, is the eighth-generation owner. He is difficult to spot among all the shelves and cupboards, but his knowledge, authority, and graciousness stand out. P. E. Guerin is the only metal foundry still in existence in twenty-first-century New York City, though the impression is of the nineteenth century. Hat pins and walking-stick handles, screws for gas lamps, and fittings for horse-drawn carriage hoods may be ordered as easily as more contemporary items: knobs, washbasin faucets, curtain rods, hinges, door handles. There are about fifty thousand articles here, in a whole host of patterns and shapes. Worn stairs of untreated wood lead up the floors to the workshops. Deep depressions in the treads evidence the boots that have trodden here daily. In the factory where the brass is cut, treated, and molded, plenty of hammering and acid-washing is taking place, to say nothing of modeling, forming, and chiseling. The air smells of burning propane, moist sand, sweat, and smoke.

Pride, an eagerness to demonstrate their handiwork, and focused concentration characterize those who work here. Each stage in the production process of each article calls for a specialist: one to make the mold, one to pour the brass, one to dry and acid wash, one to make the pattern, one to gild, and so on. Sensitive hands take care of each stage, from tracing to making an exclusive mold for each article to casting in a hole in the floor to polishing and gilding. It can take up to four months from the time the customer orders an article based on a mold or pattern until the end product is ready. Each item is cased in its own sand mold, and no mold is ever reused. Among Guerin's regular clients are a number of museums, such as the Frick Collection and the Metropolitan Museum in New York. For Heiberg Cummings, P. E. Guerin represents a historic archive and an opportunity to include period-style metalwork in the firm's interiors.

THIS FLOOR WILL
SAFELY SUSTAIN
A LOAD OF 100 LBS
PER SQUARE FOOT

ROSETTES
CHUTES
SABOTS

1321
1312

Coke

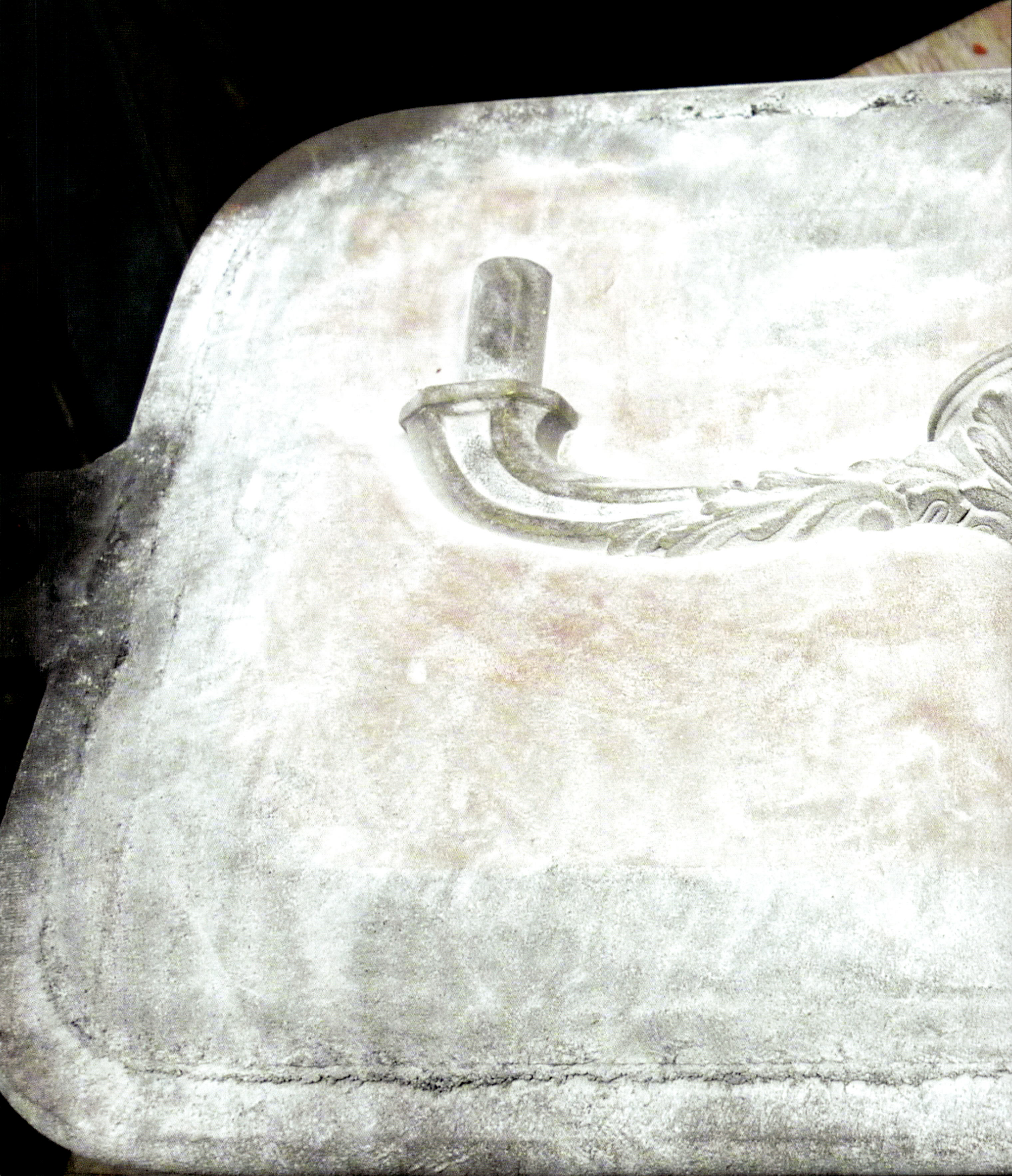

On the east coast of Long Island lies a large inland area with forest, lakes, bogs, and wetlands; it is one of the most diverse areas of fauna and flora in New York State, home to more than 125 species of birds and a host of rare flowers. By the shores of a small lake, at easy walking distance, is a majestic summer residence from the 1930s. As part of the renovatio, the designers lifted the house off its foundation and constructed a full cellar. The windows were restored to their initial form, and the original plan of rooms was retained. There is an important art collection, and the interior design allows the paintings, sculpture, and photographs to stay in focus—the muted palette does not compete with the works. The home is a cool oasis, especially when the summer heat shimmers in the air outside.

James
Brown

Navy Nurse
Anish Kapoor

KOONS

RUNAWAY
NURSE

On an icy winter's day, with frost spread over the landscape and snow crunching underfoot, a group of happy guests arrives at the elegant large house. Well-tended horses, trim of mane and gleaming of coat, stand in large outdoor paddocks; they are clad for the season in warm blankets. The guests and the large family enjoy each other's company in the stately country seat. Sitting snugly in front of an open fire, hosts and visitors enjoy the prospect of a wide park with ski tracks leading across a lake; on the far side is a large summerhouse. The large dining room with hand-painted wallpaper promotes meals distinguished by exquisite wines, delectable dishes, and stimulating conversations. Leisure pursuits, family gatherings, happy moments: the house provides a place for all.

"We develop concepts and create life experiences and histories within the field of interior design."

—Bill Cummings

In a large historic house on the western outskirts of Oslo, everything is so organized that the cook can be in the kitchen or the housekeeper at the bottom of the stairs in the basement. Today, there are no servants here. But a respect for times past has been maintained by preserving unaltered the ambience, room allocation, and history of the house. In this way, the house conveys the feeling of being drafty and rambling, with various types of windows and untouched paneling. Visitors who cross the threshold can hear the chatelaine's animated laughter as she entertains guests on the spacious terrace as hostesses have done for generations. The residence preserves and stages a dream of the harmony and formalities of bygone years.

In the winter, snow crystals cling to your eyelashes. Your cheeks glow red in the winter cold. A soft cap warms your forehead. The snow gently blankets the spruce trees. You swish off on skis with your backpack, forward toward the distant cabin. In the evenings you see the warm, welcoming light of candles through the windows as you push on through the blue winter twilight. The ski tracks point the way. The holiday cabin lies close to a large lake in Nordmarka. You ring the large iron doorbell to tell the people within you have arrived. Outside, the firewood—which promises time spent together around crackling fires—is well protected under a long roof. Inside, the fireplace is crackling and sputtering. The snow slides off your jacket and cross-country ski boots, evaporating in the indoor heat. Here it is nice and warm, and cozy in an old-fashioned way. Apparently simple, the cabin has well-chosen, exquisite, functional furniture and objects that communicate in a harmonious palette. Around the long kitchen table, the family, close friends, and friends of friends gather to plan the next ski trip or to discuss strategies for catching crawfish on warm August evenings. The conversation sparkles in time with the fire in the hearth. Soon both children and grown-ups will be playing Crazy Eights together, then the children will gather for a story-telling session before bed. They will listen half-asleep, sprawled out among the soft cushions on the bench.

KODAK 400TX

Mood and feeling.

Norway is wild and beautiful, barren and inaccessible, untouched and free. There are places where it is possible to walk for days without ever being seen by anyone. We visit cabins on vast mountain plateaus with glittering lakes or in the depths of the forest. Here we can be alone with only our nearest and dearest around us. Our roots, our family, and our childhood memories are all anchored here, among rocks and forests. The intensely dark winter nights make us conscious of the sun with its all-pervading or absent light. In a mountain cabin, a large family can gather around a spacious dining table and enjoy time together. Adults and children share a common experience in security and harmony.

"The family is surrounded by objects with a history of intimate familiarity that cuts across generations."

—Bernt Heiberg

country
NORSKE ANTIKVITETER
COLOUR

HEIBERG CUMMINGS DESIGN
NYC-OSLO
HCD3
HEIBERG CUMMINGS
OSLO • NEW YORK
ERIOR DESIGN • FURNISHINGS • ART

The Bernt and Bill Symbiosis

Øivind Storm Bjerke and Svein Olav Hoff

Øivind: When a book is going to be made about Heiberg Cummings Design, it must mean that there is something special about your work. It seems that the Bernt and Bill symbiosis is the basis of your success. It also seems as if the fact that you are so different from each other gives you a little extra to play with, from both your own perspective and that of your client. How did it all begin?

Bill: When we started twenty years ago, the office was in Oslo. We envisaged being in both Oslo and New York, but it was difficult to have two workplaces, especially in the establishing phase. Gradually, we found ourselves mostly in New York, although we held exhibitions, events, and happenings and took on design assignments in both places. Many of those who commission us come to us because they have been referred by a previous client. We are very interested in finding clients who have a synergy with what we do. If we cannot find it, we have discovered we cannot work with them. Because our job is a highly personal one, there has to be a close relation to our clients. We quite literally stick our noses into their drawers and know as much as can be known about their private lives—a relation of trust has to exist. Ninety-five percent of our assignments are private; the rest are public: restaurants, hotels, and the like.

Svein Olav: Trends come and go, but you have your own style. How do you develop your relation to the client and start work on an assignment?

Bernt: I tell clients it's important for them to volunteer as much information about themselves as possible. How do they live? What are they like? Who are they? We start there. But since many people have problems describing what sort of style they like, and what they would like to do with their surroundings, we often ask them to pick out photos of things they admire. The most important thing is to get clients to feel comfortable with themselves and with us. We probably spend more time than many other designers on the personal aspect. If you lack a good foundation, it's difficult to create something that will be perfect. There can also be disagreements between people living under the same roof about what they want. We have to take that into account, don't we? Perhaps they have just had a dispute that means that she has more latitude or vice versa: he is terribly interested, and she takes a step back. There is a lot of interaction between people. We have to pick up on that.

Svein Olav: So it is important that there is a dynamic between you, between the customers—and between you and the customer. Does the fact that there are two of you and you are so different mean that you can assume different roles in relation to the clients?

Bill: Yes, but we are pulling in the same direction, of course. Often, Bernt has a closeness to customers that I don't have. It works in various ways from client to client and becomes important as we decide which of us will run the project.

Øivind: But neither one of you has ever done a project completely on your own—there are always the two of you. Even if sometimes it is mostly Bill and at other times mostly Bernt, you're both involved in the projects, aren't you?

Bernt: Bill is a perfectionist when it comes to the architectural dimension, and I am when it comes to the aesthetic. We complement each other.

Bill: Sometimes I describe myself as a perfect imperfectionist, because I feel that the finest thing about design and life is human imperfection. You can always seek to do your best, but the result has to have a human touch—the touch of the hand. If not, it's a factory product. And even though you have the whole design concept ready, you don't want an absolutely perfect result without a trace of humanity. All the colors match, all the furniture, the hue of the wood—you know that something is missing . . .

Svein Olav: That is obvious in your interiors—there is normally something that grates somewhere, or creates some sort of insecurity.

Bernt: Yes, it's got to do with daring to do it, hasn't it?

Øivind: Is your work based on any form of theory?

Bernt: It's not about theory. I'm prepared to go so far as to state that in interior design either you have it or you don't. There are plenty of people who think you can go out and learn it. Everyone is basically capable of designing an interior. But I think we are fortunate because we have the right gene. I have a mother who inherited lots of fine things. They used to live in the attic because back then everything had to be so practical. I spent half my childhood up there, and I used to enjoy myself among the beautiful furniture making my own model houses and tableaux. I was doing this even at the age of three. It was very important for me that these were not dollhouses but model houses. My mother and father realized that they had acquired a creative little creature and let me be in peace. When the sun shone, all the other parents sent their children out to play. Mine said: "Ssh! Bernt's working. Bernt's working."

Øivind: It's interesting to look at the way you have designed the interior of a model house you still have, for it has elements of things you continue to use: decorative cushions and sofas with high backs; various textures in furniture and interiors; pictures that introduce a theme to an interior and also create a visual center of gravity, or focal point, on a wall. These are elements so evident in the model.

Bernt: I took this seriously. I made a great many model houses, but only this one has survived.

Øivind: You mentioned old things in the attic. You often introduce antiques into interiors that are otherwise characterized by new objects. Sometimes fine antiques, but also items that are more like curios that you might find at a flea market . . .

Bernt: Once, just after I went to a flea market in Nice, I flew Nice to Amsterdam, and Amsterdam to New York, with a candlestick that was larger than a machine gun in my hand luggage. I just said, "But I love candle-lit dinners." Everyone smiled and laughed—even security! That candlestick spoke to me. It had character. It was worn. It had been repaired. It cried out Bernt and Bill, and I simply had to have it home with me.

Øivind: Is there an ambition to be an artist in there somewhere?

Bernt: I'd call myself an artist.

Bill: This is where Bernt and I differ slightly. I think Bernt was born as an artist-designer. My journey has been more an amalgamation of various ideas and themes. I am interested in a lot of different topics—philosophy, religion, and other notions that pop into my head when we talk of concept. This is especially true when it has to do with stretching boundaries in the concept and also stretching boundaries in what we can do as designers. I let myself be inspired by other sciences and subject areas.

Øivind: Many people probably see Bernt as the artist and Bill as the practical one, but that is hard to swallow. It is a bit like two different stereotypes: the intellectual artist who works systematically and on the basis of principles and rules, and the more intuitive and expressionistic artist who does not base his work on a set of principles but must express things spontaneously and freely. With Bill and Bernt everything is in the same package. It's not true that there is one artist and one practical one. There are rather two different types of artistic temperament and various roles that create something unique when combined.

Bernt's family has always supported his projects. While his childhood friends played football, Bernt would construct detailed and hypermodern model houses with a sure feeling for style, trendy furnishings, and artistic decoration. Once, when his parents were away, Bernt, who was in his late teens, surprised the family by having the house painted a new color and sewing curtains for all the windows that looked symmetrical when they were seen from the front of the house. The parents were delighted when they returned home from their vacation.

~~Whether~~ When viewing spaces or objects Bill and Bernt have created or ~~create~~ while sharing an event they have produced, I have experienced ~~moments of such exultation~~ such supreme joy it has been difficult to return to my normal routine.

HEIBERG CUMMINGS
OSLO • NEW YORK

HEIBERG CUMMINGS
SIGN • FURNISHINGS • ART

In the skerries of southern Norway, a speedboat weaves its way past several small islets before reaching a sheltered modern summer house on its own island. The house is discreet and secluded, with a flawless finish and a sure-touch anchoring of original ideas. The owners, together with Bernt and Bill, have defined an interior style that is practical and functional for a family with small children as well as radically different from the "skipper houses" of the area. The family that lives here is just as much at ease on the bare rocks down by the sea as in the jungle of the metropolis—and the group thrives on challenges and excitement.

KODAK
5
5
400TX
4A

HEIBERG CUMMINGS

BEACH

EASTMAN — SAFETY — KODAK

FULTON
A
SEAMLESS
EXTRA HEAVY

FULTON
A
SEAMLESS
EXTRA HEAVY
FRANKLIN
Cane
Sugar

WESTPORT
DATTCO

Every spring, the villages of the Hamptons burst into flower. A veil of white, light pink, bright pink, or red blossoms envelops the branches of the dogwood trees. When the petals fall to the ground, they form a colorful blanket. Deer graze among the trees; large squirrels and red cardinals hop around. Large groves of cherry trees dot the local parks. Blossoming trees already many feet high are for sale at the nurseries. Broad magnolia trees with knotted trunks incline toward well-kept homes that are hundreds of years old. The small historic towns on the eastern tip of Long Island—East Hampton, Sagaponack, Water Mill, Sag Harbor, Southampton—were founded in the seventeenth century. Here lie large properties with horse paddocks and farms with orchards and organically grown vegetables. Well-tended white fences stretch as far as the eye can see. The April sun is warm and tempts visitors to sit for a long while on a bench, enjoying a mug of coffee. Lining the streets are small specialist bookstores, antiques stores, and interior design shops. Restaurants offer long, lazy meals of salad, roasted chicken, locally caught scallops, and grilled vegetables, along with a glass of white wine. Bernt and Bill commute between Manhattan and the Hamptons all year round, not only to visit with friends but to work. In fact, the Hamptons are home to a series of their interior design projects.

Whalers, seafarers, and scallop pickers walked the streets of the small towns of Martha's Vineyard and Nantucket in the nineteenth century, and many foreign languages could be heard. The crews of sailing ships toiled on the ocean no chance of communicating with the mainland. The weather-beaten, gray, shingle-clad houses had platforms on the roofs, so-called widow's walks, where the seamen's wives could keep a lookout for their husbands' ships. Beautifully items such as scrimshaw, delicate carvings from a whale bone or tooth, were crafted by those who made a living on the sea. Today on the islands residents and summer visitors cycle, meet at restaurants, sail, play tennis, fish, jog, and swim. An informal, homey lifestyle is the focus of a summer house on Martha's Vineyard. It is a place to unwind, to fill with family members from far and near, and to enjoy company during long vacation days and summer nights. In the morning, the house is immersed in a cool, impenetrable sea mist until the sun breaks through. The mist has always cloaked the island, unaffected by the passing of time or by whether it envelops the skippers of sailing ships or the pathways of modern travelers.

The endless beach stretches for mile after mile along the coast of Long Island. The sand is silver, with lapping waves, shorebirds that scurry back and forth, beautiful shells, and smooth round pebbles. The beach is alive, all year round, with sun, wind, mist, rain, snow, and ice. Here dogs run, and seals pass by during the winter. Here people are jogging, and children play and swim. Here optimists fish. When the sun sets on summer evenings, friends gaze at the shimmering colors of the sky as they dig a deep pit for a bonfire. The flames will sparkle and glow during the hours of darkness. Close at hand are beach chairs and large baskets full of drinks, food for grilling, newly picked corn, or the day's catch of scallops from the sandy sea bed. The companions sit, surrounded by laughter, conversation, good company, with perhaps a friend playing an old guitar. The stars come out in the night sky, one by one, and the moon is reflected in the water. Couples snuggle up to one another. Children doze on their parents' laps. The house has large windows with a view to the sea. The eternal breaking of the waves, a powerful sound, hangs in the air. The sand is lustrous and beautiful, its forms constantly changing. The interior highlights the sea and the colors of the beach, bringing the outside world inside. The joy and intimacy of the evening bonfire are present in the ambience of the home, and between the members of the family.

Check with Mecox they had several.

Among palm trees at the water's edge on the west coast of Florida is a Spanish Colonial–style house, built relatively recently. The verandas on the first and second floors offer relaxation in the shade of broad palm leaves—and a changing view of known and unknown captains of passing yachts. In the evening, a glowing sun slowly sinks into the Gulf of Mexico. This is a winter residence for its owners, who are deeply involved in charitable work: local social gatherings, balls, dinners, cocktail parties. Storms, tropical rain, or strong sun never prevent an atmosphere of conviviality and good humor. Here the owners can lie gently rocking in the swimming pool and at the same time study the boats as they pass close by on the broad coastal channel with its turquoise water.

A visit to an interior design showroom—any interior design showroom—with Bernt Heiberg and Bill Cummings has a certain shape and constancy. The pair are good customers, and loyal ones. Always there is an effusive greeting: "Bernt and Bill, how nice to see you!" Always there is a warm exchange with a young man or woman: "You look wonderful! Did you change your hair? Such a nice tan, where have you been?" Always there are kisses—more than one, in the European fashion—and hugs. A visit to select curtains, cushions, and furniture for a client with an apartment in downtown New York is no different.

The task appears to be insurmountable—there are thousands of fabric samples hanging close together, and the choice is going to take hours. But Bernt has a sure eye for quality, structure, and color combinations. He rushes between the shelves, holding his dog Flink in his arms. "Do you like this one?" he asks Flink, who yawns his approval. Then Bernt starts to pull out the samples, one bay at a time, reaching with a sure hand into the over-full racks. First comes thin, transparent linen in a shade of muted beige, then fuzzy mohair in a cream tone for a cushion, soft velvet in a light blue-gray for the edge of a dining-table chair, and finally a rough, blue-striped cotton. "That's for a low bench," Bernt explains.

Meanwhile, Bill has drifted to the outer edge of the showroom. "There's a coffee table here," he calls across the large room. The table has iron legs of unsymmetrical thickness and a top of thick wood with inlaid circles of the same type of wood. It is handmade and unique, like a special item of jewelry. The top is sanded and bleached. "Perfect. We need a ceiling light as well," Bernt says. In the corner, among an array of crystal chandeliers, hangs a huge lantern, heavy and made of large plates of glass. The lamp is in subtle tones of pale blue and gray-blue, like the sea in a mist and, when lit, bears a resemblance to a magic paper lantern. Iron weaves its way between the surfaces and conveys an impression of a glass mosaic. "We've got to have that," Bernt says at once.

The pile of linen, cotton, and velvet; the circles of the table-top: it all hangs together. It is like an unassembled jigsaw puzzle in which the pieces have a certain cohesion even though the picture has not yet been completed. The color of the velvet is reflected in the lamp. The soft, round weave of the mohair is taken up in the tabletop. The hard iron of the lamp relates to the legs of the coffee table. And the discreet blue shades are repeated and juggled in the cushions and the curtains. For the thin linen is not actually beige. It is an ever so faint gray-steel-blue, a tone that is brought out by the color of the lamp and the cushions.

"And then we need chairs," Bill says, "don't we, Flink?" Flink, now in Bill's arms, has fallen asleep. The two partners comb the seemingly hundreds of different types of armchair in the showroom. Bill assesses one of them. "I don't think so," Bernt says. "Okay," responds Bill. Bernt comments, "I feel like sinking into one of the chairs." "No, not that one," Bill protests. "You can sit down in those two," he says, pointing at them. Behind a shelf, forgotten and off the beaten track, stand two chairs. They look as if someone forgot them in the 1920s. They are low, with oval backs, deep cushions, and straight, dark legs. The oval shape repeats the circles in the tabletop and the scrolling iron of the lamp. "Those we must have," Bernt and Bill cry out in unison. "We'll recover them with a deep, rough gray-blue-green velvet and use water-blue and corn-ear-pale cushions." "But we need a red cushion as well," Bill adds, "to remind the client that this is a home where she's expected to have some fun and let her hair down. We like to include an unanticipated element that reinforces the client's personality and the design concept at the same time."

The designers leave a long order and, after another exchange of kisses, zoom down in the elevator. "Flink needs his lunchtime walk," Bernt and Bill say with a smile. "Have a nice and creative day," the doorman says as he holds open the glass doors. And just like that, the two walk into the yellow taxicab chaos of Manhattan, with Flink wagging his tail alongside.

POST CARD

The owners of an apartment overlooking Central Park look forward to exploring Manhattan as a married couple and as a family with children. Here they can live in a challenging way, seeking out activities they do not experience in Oslo and learning about new aspects of art, sport, and culture. Experiencing and breaking new ground—the interdependence between family and friends—is what is in focus.

IMPORTANT WORKS OF ART ACTUALLY "WORK" TO ARTICULATE AN IDEA OF THE SACRED IN OUR WORLD.

CALLUM INNES 2007

The many projects Heiberg Cummings Design has completed in Manhattan are spread out over large parts of the island. New York City stimulates and appeals to all the senses. Ever present are intense smells, sense impressions, suggestive noises: you hear the hooting of taxicabs, the fire truck finding its way through dense traffic with its sirens wailing, the garbage collectors rattling large lids. Tango evenings, regattas, Thai cookery courses, graffiti, birdwatching, trapeze training, instruction in mime: nothing is unattainable. The virtually impossible just takes a bit more time. If a man dressed as a radish wanders down the street, you don't even bother to look. Individuality and creativity, trying to realize your personal dream, are appreciated and encouraged. *If I can make it there, I'll make it anywhere*, Liza Minnelli sings. Each neighborhood—even each micro-neighborhood consisting of just a few blocks—has a strong feeling of identity. At the dry cleaner they remember your name the second time you come. In the juice bar they welcome you back, even though you've been away for five months. The man in the newspaper kiosk calls out to you when the magazine you like to read has arrived.

How you experience Manhattan differs a great deal, in large part depending on where your home is. You enter the neighborhood and you leave the neighborhood; the few blocks you move within every day characterize your daily routine and are most important for your perception of New York City. Your home is a nest in a tree with many branches; the neighborhood—and the way in which you are a part of it—makes up a significant part of your everyday life. Your neighborhood is both a safe anchorage and a portal to endless possibilities.

You generally walk or take a bus, cab, or the subway; you rarely drive. You buy food and carry it home from the same shop, greet the same people sitting out on benches, make conversation with your neighbors in the elevator in the same way every single day. You disappear below ground to the intense squealing of subway tracks. You whoosh upward in a skyscraper and marvel at how anyone has managed to cart beds, large dining tables, and sofas in such a tiny elevator. Once, in order to install a large dining table in a converted workshop on the third floor of a building in Soho, Heiberg Cummings had to hire an enormous crane and remove an expansive window to get the piece of furniture inside. When furnishing an apartment on the thirty-eighth floor of an apartment building, the designers employed specialists to transport the pieces on the roof of the elevator.

In a penthouse apartment, you are met by silence. You look up at the sky and down at the roofs and even farther down at the streets where yellow cabs look like tiny moving building blocks. Perhaps you can make out the Hudson River to the west, with its ferry traffic and Statue of Liberty like a small doll in the distance, or the East River to the east, across to Queens and Long Island and the airports with their dense traffic and airplanes that look like large birds against the sky. You are never idle: something is going on around the clock. *I want to wake up in a city that never sleeps*, Frank Sinatra sings.

CORNELIA PARKER - ALTER EGO 2010

BOYD WEBB - BE

ED WINDOW 2010

GENE DAVIS "BLUE CLOUD"

1983-2006

2004
TERRY WINTERS - INDIGO SEQUENCE / 5

HEATHER ROWE - THE THI

VIKRAM
SETH
CHESS
STEFAN
ZWEIG

The apartment is on the thirtieth floor of a Manhattan skyscraper. Large windows face northwest, and Central Park is visible in the distance. Below are private roofs with terraces covered with flowers, parasols, and outdoor furniture, undisturbed oases far above the noise and bustle of the streets. In the evening, as the sun sets, the light shimmers blue. The owner is slender and elegant, spontaneous and reflective. The titles on her bookshelves bear witness to her interests and profession as a psychologist: *Going to Pieces without Falling Apart, Starving to Death in a Sea of Objects, The Good Karma Divorce, Yoga and the Quest for the True Self,* and *The Life and Work of Sigmund Freud.* A broad desk sits in a spacious area. The furniture reflects the character of the owner: delicate, refined, embracing, inclusive. She says, "I decided to convert the whole apartment, to renovate and replace fabrics and furniture shortly after my husband died. He was my great love. We met each other in our late forties. I cannot envision ever living with another man. But I don't want to live in a memorial grove and keep the interior exactly as it was. With Bill and Bernt's help I have made the apartment a place where I can create a new existence as a single person and be happy growing old alone. I am not keeping a place open for a new man—I had to create surroundings where I could get back to just being me." Her relationship with the designers began while she was married. That was when Bernt and Bill renovated the apartment for the first time. The relationship is based on trust, and she freely talks about the friendship that has evolved among the three. "They helped me develop in a new direction, take up new challenges. At the same time, I noticed that my preferences were changing and that I was pushing my own borders," she comments. The designers changed the floor plan so that the living room, study, and bedroom are laid out on an axis along the windows. Sliding doors with rectangular fields of dark wood partition off the three rooms. The concept—a home for contemplation, innovation, and energy—is reflected in the subdued palette of colors and in surprising elements such as an enormous urn on a small, delicate table or a table where the legs swirl in a spiral. The backs of the rococo-style armchairs are upholstered in checkered silk ticking. In the bedroom is an exquisite Art Deco make-up table with inset mirrors. Bill and Bernt have captured the owner's elegance as well as her wish for security and renewal.

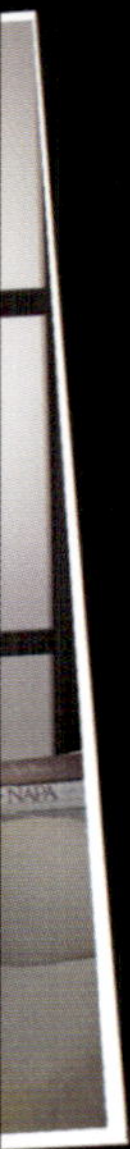

“Their style and genius is to connect with the client. They helped me to evolve and sent me in the right direction.”

—Ellen Robinson

In a large penthouse apartment in Soho, in lower Manhattan, hangs an exquisite collection of photographs. The quality of the collection is such that many museums might well envy its owner, an international and knowledgeable connoisseur of historic and contemporary photographs. Here visitors are entertained, here art-related issues are discussed, and here the owner can surround himself with his photographic images.

universal

HEIBERG CUMMINGS

Men Without

SPAS
Africa
VANITAS
MAPPLETHORPE

IY 5053
KODAK TMY 5053
KODAK TMY 5053
12A
13
13A
KODAK TMY 5053
0049

KODAK TMY 5053
13A
14
14A
Y 5053

Shaking Things Up

Øivind Storm Bjerke and Svein Olav Hoff

Øivind: Have you ever entered a specific situation with the express intention of shaking things up? The question is a natural one for you given the event that took place at Kaare Berntsen, one of Norway's premiere art and antique galleries, shortly after the gallery moved to new premises. It could seem as if both of you were attempting to get the gallery to abandon ingrown habits and at the same time wanting to give the viewing public a new awareness of how an art gallery can be experienced by creating a new atmosphere. This new awareness is perhaps radically different from what has been inherited from the gallery's history. Was it a conscious strategy on your part?

Bill: Yes, and what was so tremendously inspiring was the enthusiasm the staff showed. It seemed as though we had given them license to break out of conventional ways of presenting art and antiques.

Svein Olav: When I arrived, I was met with a "lovely to see you again" and a hug from a young hostess. My immediate thought was: But I don't know you. Everything that took place followed a carefully planned script in which the public were co-actors. Once a customer had become part of the setting, it almost felt like being at a cocktail party that could have taken place around 1962, possibly not in Oslo, but in some other place from our collective fantasy. But why?

Bill: The important thing was not to link it to a particular period but to use the transposition in time to encourage the public to think about what is happening and what they are doing in this setting. The public connects with certain types of objects presented in certain ways at sales exhibitions. Kaare Berntsen is a well-known antiques dealer. By making use of elements that many people would not associate with design and, more specifically, contemporary design, we hoped to stimulate the conversation about what defines modern design. Are the traditional definitions still valid?

Svein Olav: One of the most striking elements was a generously laid-out table with a couple sitting one at each end. They sat there eating, without talking to each other—what was the idea behind this?

Bernt: To start with, the presentation in itself was a still life—one of our hallmarks. The still life is an object in the interior, but at the same time it is a living object. The people were objects just as the candlesticks, chairs, and pictures were objects. That was why we didn't want them to create a drama out of the situation. That they do not speak was an important point. I ought perhaps to add that the sumptuousness of such an interior can take over, and that those living there perhaps do not have anything to talk about with each other. They are so far from each other that they are disconnected.

Svein Olav: The composition is baroque, but it also has an element of stringency about it.

Bill: Yes, great stringency, but at the same time it crosses all the boundaries when it comes to style, period, and the idea of what can be considered an object within a contemporary interior.

Svein Olav: The composition is baroque, but it also has an element of stringency about it.

Bill: Yes, great stringency, but at the same time it crosses all the boundaries when it comes to style, period, and the idea of what can be considered an object within a contemporary interior.

Kultur

GRESK BRYLLUPSROMANTIKK: Hellas' prins Nikolaos (bildet) giftet seg i går med sin Tatiana Blatnik. De nygifte vinket til gjestene fra kirketrappa og klinte til med et kyss for de frammøtte fotografene. Kronprins Haakon var blant gjestene i bryllupet.

NÆR ENIGHET I TV 2: Ledelsen i TV 2 tror en ny konsesjonsavtale snart kan underskrives. Kulturminister Anniken Huitfeldt (bildet) gir TV 2 selv skylden for at forhandlingene har tatt lang tid. – Forsinkelsene skyldes at TV 2, etter eget ønske, ville ha en pause i forhandlingene fra april til 23. juni, sier Huitfeldt (Ap).

Når gode designråd er dyre

Fiffen festet som det va

De bruker et år på å designe hjemmet ditt, og har blant annet en av verdens rikeste og Stein Erik Hagen på kundelista. I går arrangerte Heiberg og Cummings retrofest for Oslo-fiffen.

RETROFEST

Tekst: **Geir Ramnefjell**
ger@dagbladet.no

Innleide skuespillere er kledd opp for å simulere at vi er i 1962, og møter gjestene når de går opp den røde løperen utenfor kunsthandler Kaare Berntsens gedigne murvilla – et steinkast fra Aker Brygge i Oslo.

– Det er jo blitt mer vanlig i utlandet at for eksempel kunstnere, arkitekter og designere samarbeider om å lage en happening som virkelig sitter, sier Bernt Heiberg.

Sammen med partner og kollega Bill Cummings har de to designet hjemmene til en rekke velstående mennesker både i USA og Norge.

I sommer etablerte de et større kontor i Oslo, og i går hadde de fest der deres kundekrets og Kaare Berntsens kundekrets fikk se kunsthandlerens antikviteter og kunstverk i en litt spesiell ramme – dandert av Heiberg Cummings. De har plassert seg midt i trendbildet med å skru klokke tilbake til 1962, med filmen "A Single Man" som referansepunkt.

– Vi vil gi folk en forestilling, gjøre det til en happening, forklarer Heiberg.

Kom, så, kjøpte

Det fikk de. Investor Ola Mæle og kona Vibeke Mæle hilser pent på skuespillerparet som utgir seg for å være herr og fru Heftye – og kveldens vertskap.

Stein Erik Hagen og kona Mille-Marie Treschow sier pent farvel til det samme skuespillerparet i det de forlater villaen – med forsikringer om at de har kjøpt.

– Heiberg og Cummings er gode venner av oss, vet du. Bare morsomt med skuespillerne. Det er flere inne, sier Hagen til Dagbladet før han setter seg inn i bilen ved siden av sjåføren, mens kona setter seg baksetet.

Inne går en kvinnelig servitør i 60-tallssnitt utstudert, og helt alene, sakte opp og ned trappa med et brett dry martinis. I et annet rom sitter et skuespillerpar og spiser middag ved et overdådig middagsbord, som en slags kunstinstallasjon.

Heiberg og Cummings har gjort tilsvarende eventer i New York. Men der arrangerer de også andre kunstutstillinger, blant annet med Munch – der en av verdens rikeste finansmenn, George Soros, var blant gjestene.

– He's a very nice guy, sier Cummings.

Nettverksbygging

For det er tross alt kontakter og nettverksbygging festen handler om. Interiørdesignerne har en svært velstående kundekrets, men den er liten – og må pleies.

– Dette er reklame for alle parter. Våre kunder er litt de samme som Kaare Berntsens. De har litt ålreit økonomi, og er kunst og kulturinteresserte. Og i det siste er interiør blitt veldig populært blant de unge, så det ser vi mer av nå, sier Heiberg.

Navnene til kundene vil de helst holde tett om.

– Vi bruker omtrent et år på å

ANGEL: Diandra Douglas går rettens vei
sent av Michael Douglas' (bildet) ho-
nye filmen «Money Never Sleeps». Da de
ngikk de en avtale som ga eks fru Douglas
på en del av pengene eksmannen tjente.
Kultur 39
k Hagen og kona Mille-Marie Treschow var
estene som kom. Foto: John T. Pedersen
PRIVATSJÅFØR: Ola og Vibeke
Mæle kom med privatsjåfør.
Foto: John T. Pedersen
FAKTA
Heiberg og Cummings
Designerparet Bernt Heiberg og Bill Cummings.
Designer interiør for en velstående kundekrets, i Norge og utenlands.
Har jobbet sammen i 20 år, og har kontor i New York og Oslo. I sommer oppgraderte de virksomheten i Oslo.
962
det er klart at her skapes det et sjikt som redefinerer sin kultur ved å kjøpe smak de ikke har. Og at Heiberg og Cummings framhever kunstnerisk ekspertise, er heller ikke tilfeldig, mener Tangen.
– Når kulturelle mennesker skal ha en middag, liker de å ha en utlending med i selskapet. Og når rike mennesker skal ha middag, vil de ha en kunstner der – som de føler de kan være på likefot med.

Hitherto it has been assumed that all our knowledge must conform to objects. But all attempts to establish something about them a priori by means of concepts, and thus to expand our knowledge, have on this supposition come to nothing. We should therefore attempt to tackle the task of metaphysics more successfully by assuming that the objects must conform to our knowledge.

Up to now it has been assumed that all our cognition must conform to the objects; but all attempts to find out something about them a priori through concepts that would extend our cognition have, on this presupposition, come to nothing. Hence let us once try whether we do not get farther with the problems of metaphysics by assuming that the objects must confirm to our cognition.

Immanuel Kant, *Critique of Pure Reason, Preface to the Second Edition*

Throughout history humankind has had a need to cultivate meaning and an idea of the sacred within the immediate environment. This manifested itself in ancient times in works of art and objects that focused, articulated, and illuminated ideas of the sacred within a culture. These ideas were contemplated, preserved, and passed down through generations by an elite class. Cultures were cohesive and were able to establish common ideals based on such works of art and architecture.

The practice of imparting meaning into people's lives from the top down persisted in Western culture until the advent of the Renaissance, when a trend toward a multiplicity of sources for meaning and the idea of the sacred developed, although it was still not prevalent. During the long period between the Renaissance and the late nineteenth century, a network of specialty craft guilds grew out of the demand for objects of art and utility that held within their nature the idea of the sacred. These guilds stemmed from the need to protect methods of production as well as the visions and insights that were refined over multiple generations of apprenticeship.

The guild system cultivated and preserved technical skills that gave its members an advantage over those who were not part of a such a group. But more important than the skills that were generated was an unintended by-product of this way of working: a special ability to see qualities and values within the raw materials that were used in a given craft or vocation. This ability to see things in the world that others could not was enhanced through the traditions of apprenticeship. When young artisans practiced alongside masters who had worked a craft for many years, they learned, through a process of trial and error, to discern differences among the raw materials they were working with.

In *The Wheelwright's Shop*, published in 1923, George Sturt writes about the craft of the wheelwright, the guild that constructed wagon wheels for carriages. Sturt notes that the craftsmen had reverence for the wood they worked with, as well as reverence for the countryside where the trees were grown. The wrights had the talent to see qualities in the wood that came from working the material with their hands and used the ability to see such nuances to apply the materials to their best use. Because the materials were always different, presenting different opportunities and different obstacles, the methods of cultivating them at their best were also always different. It must necessarily be so.

RICHARD SERRA
THE MATTER OF TIME
PENGUIN CLASSICS
IMMANUEL KANT
Critique of Pure Reason
TIMBER: BUYING

Sturt writes further, however, that the ability to see these subtle qualities was under attack from the advent of technologies such as the electric band saw and other woodworking machines. These machines separated the craftsman from the material that they were working with and, by so doing, made them less able to see the virtues in the wood and less able to produce a product of the highest quality.

Even though the ability to discern qualities has been diminished in the contemporary world, humanity still possesses the potential to actualize this vision through practice, trial and error, and a sincere interest in bringing out the best result. We can see this vision in the sailboat captain who recognizes a wind not just as a current of air but as a special type of air flow having direction and strength, requiring a particular strategy or tack to arrive at the desired location. We can see it too in the photographer who doesn't just record an object with the push of a button but instead identifies the way the light reacts with the subject and how the subject relates to its environment within a composition.

The world of environmental design has experienced similar challenges to the focus and integrity of the craft. At the end of the nineteenth century, designers, riding the wave of the industrial revolution, saw the opportunities of mass production and began producing objects, textiles, and furnishings at an unprecedented level. Everything suddenly became decorated, and thus was born the gilded age.

Because of the overproduction of material goods, thinkers, designers, and architects tried to clean up the clutter of meaningless objects by embracing the new idea of modernism. But rather than returning to the philosophy of craft, they decided that designers should embrace the idea of the efficiency of the machine in an effort to cultivate meaning and focus only on the elements of people's lives that are functionally relevant, drawing on the idea that Le Corbusier heralded, that a home should be a machine.

Designers and architects took this thought process to its natural conclusion and discovered that pure functionalism, brought about through the processes of mass production, didn't bring either meaning or an idea of the sacred into individuals' lives. Quite the contrary, it left humankind empty and cold.

In this pursuit of meaning in contemporary life, designers abandoned the ideals of modernism but maintained the practice of mass production and moved into the current era, which has been called postmodernism. In an effort to bring individuality back into the present day, designers discovered that through technology and with computer-generated design multiples of similar elements could be produced as inexpensively as multiples of identical elements. Consequently, consumers are now being bombarded with objects of mass reproduction in which the distinctions between authentic and inauthentic, between real and imagined, and between meaningful and inconsequential are blurred.

We now live in a world where on one day the best design accomplishments are rewarded and on the next day those same items are produced by others in China and sold at a fraction of the price of the original. Where and how is value discerned? How do we bring back meaning and an idea of the sacred in our environment? What happens to us now?

Perhaps the answer to these questions may be found in the ancient Greek idea of poiesis and poietic style. The term is derived from a Greek term meaning "to make." (It is also the root of our modern "poetry.") According to H. D. F. Kitto in *Poiesis: Structure and Thought*, "Aristotle's dictum [states] that the most important element in poiesis is the arrangement of the material; and by this is meant not simply giving a more or a less elegant shape to something which in either case remains virtually the same thing, but that the arrangement is itself, in the hands of a good poet."

The word *poiesis*, which incorporates the ideas of both creation and vision, opens a treasure trove of possible applications in the pursuit of greater meaning in our environment. Just as the wheelwright honed technical skills as well as an ability to see qualities in materials and the environment, so can we view our creative life as a craft in the same way. If we turn this attitude to design, it refocuses our efforts away from purely physical goals and instead toward goals of cultivating greater poietic meanings in our lives. Furthermore, this view of the creative process as craft implies not only that meanings are revealed in objects but also that objects reveal meanings in their creator.

The establishment of these meanings in our environment takes three forms: *objective meanings*, *ritualistic meanings*, and *practical meanings*. When discussing *objective meanings* it is important to understand the context within which a relationship to an external object exists. It can be difficult to understand how objects around us can have any intrinsic meaning. After all, an object is just a thing. Aside from the desire we may have to own something due to a particular function or use that an object may serve, how can an object have any real meaning? For something to have meaning there must be some sort of internal connection with it.

It is worth considering the anthropic principle, which states, most simply, that conditions observed in the universe must be compatible with the observer of those conditions. This principle, which has applications in both philosophy and physics, implies that there is a dependent relationship between external objects and our knowledge and perception of them. Immanuel Kant discusses this relationship in his *Critique of Pure Reason*, in which he says, "space is not an empirical concept which has been derived from outer experiences." By this he means that space is not a concept that is determined from observing the external world. It is rather an internal intuition or rule that we use to make sense of the world around us. He maintains that if this statement is true, it is the external world that conforms to our understanding of it and not the other way around.

If we apply Kant's understanding to our personal environments, it becomes clear that it is up to the individual to discover internally how we project meaning into the objects around us. In other words, it is a cultivation of a vision not of the external world but of our internal intuitions.

Bill's Perfect Martini

Ingredients & Equipment:

* Room temperature Hendrick's Gin or Ketel One Vodka

* Ice cubes made of filtered or distilled water

* Martini & Rossi Dry Vermouth

* **Manzanilla Olives:** Spanish green olive, unpitted, lightly lye-cured then packed in salt and lactic acid brine

* A **cocktail glass:** A stemmed glass which has a cone-shaped bowl placed upon a stem above a flat base. The stem allows the drinker to hold the glass without affecting the temperature of the drink, and the wide bowl places the surface of the drink directly under the drinker's nose, ensuring that the aromatic element has the desired effect.

* Cobbler Shaker: A three-piece cocktail shaker that has tapers at the top and ends with a built-in strainer and includes a cap.

* Silver cocktail stick: A short cylindrical stick, made of silver, that has a somewhat sharp point on both ends. It is used as a skewer for Olives in the cocktail.

Directions:

Take two Olives and skew them with the cocktail stick and place into the freezer for one hour.

Freeze the glass so that it becomes frosty white when it comes into contact with the room air. If you plan to become a frequent drinker of Martinis, regularly storing the glasses in the freezer is a very convenient way to be prepared. You can keep them in their box.

Pour 75ml (or approx 2+ 1/2 oz) of room temperature Gin or vodka and 3 drops of Dry Vermouth into the shaker. After doing this a couple of times you will no longer find it necessary to measure. Measuring is actually rather bad form.

Then throw a half dozen ice cubes into the shaker, close the lid and shake vigorously until white frost forms on the exterior of the shaker. This process can sometimes take nearly a minute and can be painful to your hand due to the cold temperature. Often times I wrap the shaker in a hand towel to shield my hand from the cold frost.

At this point the glass should be removed from the freezer and the frosted skewered olives placed in the glass. Then remove the cap from the shaker and pour the frozen cocktail into the frosty glass.

Serve immediately! The first sip is sublime and sets the drinker's mood so that the entire cocktail can be experienced properly.

To cite a practical example, when set to the task of selecting objects to go into composing a room, it is important to examine the qualities that those objects possess and how their poietic meanings relate to each other to create a narrative. The physical aspects of the selection process take on a secondary importance. An antique piece of ceramic that shows the signs of use and even areas of repair has a particular story. It could be placed alongside other objects with a similar story or alongside objects that have a different story or even no story at all. The process of putting objects together is not about matching their physical characteristics but rather about blending their poietic meanings.

When examining objects to be included in a personal space it is important to be as inclusive as can be imagined. We should not only attempt to discover meanings in obvious objects—sofas, chairs, and tables—but should also consider elements within the larger environment such as new or existing structures (houses or buildings); the empty space between objects; the culture within which objects exist; and people themselves in relation to objects, both animate and inanimate. All of these elements have potential meanings and qualities that can be examined and revealed just as a large rusted Richard Serra sculpture can. Serra is world renowned for creating monumental steel sculptures that encourage the viewer to enter and move around in a way that focuses attention on the spaces defined by the sculpture. In his essay "Notes on the Matter of Time," Serra states, "The meaning of the installation will be activated and animated by the rhythm of the viewer's movement. Meaning occurs only through continuous movement, through anticipation, observation, and recollection." In this same interactive way meanings are cultivated within our own spaces. And once they are revealed, just as in the wheelwrights' traditions, these qualities can be put to their best use to create an environment characterized by poietic meanings.

In addition to the intrinsic meanings/qualities that objects may possess, there are also objects that support *ritualistic meanings* in our lives. By this I mean that there are objects within our environments that hold poietic meanings only to the extent that they facilitate a meaningful activity in our lives.

For example, many people enjoy the idea of having a cocktail after work. In my particular case, I am fond of a martini after a day of work or play. But what is it about this ritualistic activity that gives meaning to my life? How do I know that this is not simply a habit or even an addiction? If we examine the activity in terms of what its substitutions may be, and if any of the substitutions prove to be an acceptable alternative, then perhaps the activity may in fact be habitual. However, if the substitution is not found to be an acceptable alternative, then the activity in question may be seen as poieticly meaningful. And if it can be determined that there exists some meaning in an activity, then this meaning can be refined into a ritual that provides an idea of the sacred, albeit in small degree. Finally, if we can, by replication, examine and develop a variety of different small activities in this same way, we could then cultivate a life rich with poietic meaning.

It is easy to see how this example may work in our everyday life. My goal of the cocktail is not to attain a state of intoxication. If it were, I could simply drink a glass of vodka. To the extent that

I do not find that to be an appealing alternative, it becomes evident that there exists some meaning in the activity. When making a martini, I like a shaken cocktail consisting of ice made of filtered water, a drop of chilled vermouth, and a shot of room temperature vodka or gin. I like to have the cocktail served in a frozen stemmed glass with an inverted conical vessel.

How is it that an individual can be so specific about a small ritualistic activity? This personal knowledge comes only through trial and error. If I had not once prepared a martini using frozen vodka, I would not have discovered that frozen vodka would not melt the ice cubes and thus the drink would be composed of pure vodka. If I had not experimented with different shaped glasses, I would not have discovered the perfect shape and size to maximize my experience with this ritual.

When we ponder how a small ritual affects poietic meaning within our environment, we need only examine where we find ourselves when performing any meaningful activity. In the case of my martini, I love to sit on the terrace and watch the sun set. I therefore have chairs on the terrace with well-worn arms upon which I can set my cocktail. Objects in my environment are arranged so as to best bring out meanings in this ritual as well as my other rituals and the rituals of my family.

This brings us back to the point that people should be considered important animated objects to be integrated into a meaningful environment. People may be thought to be intrinsic objects, and they may also be thought to be part of a meaningful ritual. For instance, there are times when coming together with our families or friends can be a meaningful and sacred activity. It is essential to consider how these people are brought into an environment that is rich with meaning.

It is important to remember that it is unrealistic to think that it is possible to construct an environment in which every object radiates profound meaning and every activity within that environment touches the soul in some deep way. To do so would mean that we would live in a world disconnected from the full spectrum of humanity. There are always going to be objects that are meaningless, technologies that diminish our creative practices of seeing and cultivating meaning, and people with whom we come into contact that do not enrich us in any way and may, in fact, deplete our souls. To think that we can make the world otherwise would be delusional.

To deal with this negative aspect of our environment it is vital to develop within ourselves the ability to embrace *practical meanings* in our world. This means to develop in ourselves the ability to incorporate into our lives meaningless objects, rituals, and people without embracing the way of life that they represent. No one other than a cloistered monk or a solitary hermit can experience even a single day without encountering meaninglessness. Even if we were able to construct such detached lives for ourselves, this would come at the cost of excluding that which is human. We would lose our humanity.

The practice of cultivating practical meanings involves, once again, the ability to see various degrees of meaning in our world. Hubert Dreyfus and Sean Dorrance Kelly write in *All Things Shining* that what is "even worse than losing quality . . . is losing the skill for telling the difference." Their

point is that if we learn to discern a difference in quality, we can accept and compartmentalize objects of lesser quality in our environment. While this may sound like a compromise leading to mediocrity, it is just the opposite.

Those of us who strive for excellence when constructing an environment come into situations where we are confronted with limitations to our choices, limitations based on budgets, accessibility, disagreements, and so on. Even in the most favorable circumstances constraints are still present. Although we may have improved the ability to discern distinctions of quality, worth, and meaningfulness, we are nevertheless compelled by circumstances to make selections of objects of lesser meaning and quality. The craft lies in how objects of lesser quality are integrated into an overall environment that is rich with poietic meanings. Thus the task is not to eliminate the meaningless elements in an environment but to give those elements their proper voice in the concept of the environment as a whole.

When furnishing a room we are constantly bombarded with images of styles, environments, and objects indicative of our age of mass reproduction. Restoration Hardware's reproduction collections, for instance, are a tempting idea for the price-conscious consumer. It may seem that selecting a picture in the catalog and having the various pieces delivered is an efficient way to furnish a room. However, working in this way removes the craft and thereby any poietic meaning in the environment. This is not to say that an inexpensive piece devoid of intrinsic meanings cannot be used as an element within a poieticly meaningful environment. But we must be selective about its use, keeping resources focused on objects that have greater objective or ritualistic meanings.

Poiesis in Action

It wasn't until we started working on this book that we discovered what it is that we actually do. Interior design. What is that? Why would someone want to make a book about what we have done? What is it that is relevant about what we do? Who wants to pay the certain number of dollars or pounds that were paid to experience this book?

These questions sparked an internal exploration. There must be an answer, a good answer, to these questions if there is going to be any relevance to this book. John Lennon once said, "Life is what happens to you while you're busy making other plans." This is so true in our case. We have been so busy doing what we do that we haven't had the opportunity to step back and see it for ourselves.

Bernt Heiberg and I started our collaboration in the spring of 1990. The Berlin Wall had just fallen, and the world was in a transformative mood. Old institutions were dissolving; new structures were being conceived to fill the void. We met in Warsaw, Poland, in the most unlikely of circumstances and felt an immediate kinship: an American and a Norwegian; two creative souls excited about the possibilities ahead and eager to construct a new way of thinking about design and the environment.

Bernt, an extroverted artist/antique dealer, and I, an introverted actor/photographer, started our company with the naïve conviction that we would only work with white. While we now look at that moment with amusement, it is nevertheless true that there could have been no better blank canvas for us to start developing our method of working. In retrospect, we were an unlikely pair, souls of different cultures and perspectives, cultivating a system that accommodates both structure and emotion.

Our relationship with the client has always been one of a very personal nature. Bernt has the innate ability to see into the nature of people and to get them to reveal what is meaningful in their lives; I have been the one to give structure to these meanings. Together, we interpret and incorporate these meanings into our environments.

Because of our non-classical background, free of institutional certifications and judgments, we naturally and unintentionally originated a parallel process of working. This dual-process method addresses the practical physical aspects of running a project as well as the poietic and meaningful aspects. Whether apparent or not to the client, these two processes are conducted simultaneously over the course of a project.

Although every project is different and the phases of development vary, they all tend to have some common and universal elements. Four basic phases of work—the first meeting phase, the presentation phase, the execution phase, and the installation phase—illustrate the dual processes that exist in each of them.

On the physical and practical level, the first meeting phase includes such activities as a survey and review of the scope of work, a determination of the client's objectives, and a review of the style of the structure and existing furnishings and objects. However, on the poietic level we are beginning a process of positive disintegration. We attempt to discern the basic elements of the client's aesthetic. We try to separate ideas of fashion from personal taste, cultural beliefs from personal values, and habits from rituals. This exploration is generally conducted on a subliminal level while the principal analysis is focused on the physical activities.

After we have reviewed and agreed on the scope and goals of a project, we are ready to start working. This second stage of a project we call the presentation phase. This is where we structure a concept and specify the elements that go into the design. We engage the client by asking him or her to contribute images from magazines or ideas that have been experienced in travels or in home life. Once the client's input has been integrated into our concepts we make a style presentation that the client either confirms or modifies. Once the style is established, we assemble the specifications that will compose the physical design and make a final presentation to the client for approval. But this is just the physical.

On the poietic level of the presentation phase, we are working toward evolving imagination and creativity within the client. We direct our conversations to gain clues as to where poietic meaning may lie within his or her existing environment as well as the imagined environment. While we are exploring with the client, we as the designers are also undergoing an evolution: we are opening our imagination to adopt the client's perspective. Seeing the world from another's outlook allows for the discovery of new possibilities and unique constellations of elements. In this phase, it is important not to allow the creative process to be harnessed by our will. We work toward being open to collaborative exploration with the client.

Once the designs are completed and approved, we move into the execution phase of the project. Drawings and specifications are delivered to contractors and craftspeople so that they may begin their work. Furnishings are put into production. Textiles are ordered and shipped to various workrooms for fabrication. Follow-up protocols are set into action to make sure that all the elements are where they should be at any given time. This is the most physically challenging phase of a project, because at this point so many different people are involved, and they all have to be orchestrated to achieve the same end. The most important member of this orchestra is the client, who on the poietic level is undergoing a maturation process with regard to design. Conceptions are evolving into realities, and as these realities start to take form, poietic meanings begin to reveal themselves. These meanings may or may not be as expected. The project may present unexpected challenges and/or opportunities. The expectations must then be cultivated within the client and the designer to bring the best to this dynamic phase of the project.

Once all the elements of a project have been fabricated, sewn, constructed, refinished, and so on, we are ready for the installation phase. On the physical level this is simply putting everything in its place and styling it so that it looks beautiful. It is a bigger job than it sounds, but it is a straightforward one. On the other hand, on the poietic level this is the most creative and important phase of any project. Here we take the objective, ritualistic, and practical meanings that have been revealed over the course of the project and utilize them to create an environment full of meaning. Even though plans, renderings, and drawings have all been done, at this stage we endeavor to free ourselves from these constraints and allow the environment to evolve with reference to the revealed meanings. We strive to be free to experiment, and by so doing we are able to integrate both the structure and the functionality that come from the physical planning with the meanings that have been uncovered.

The final result will be unique, and it will show little physical relationship to other projects, but on the poietic level the process is always the same. We and our client collaborators learn to see new poietic meanings in objects within our environment that we were unable to see before. The more sincerely we practice poiesis the more we see and the more profoundly we enrich our souls. Ultimately, this is the highest goal that creative work can aspire to.

Although the exam period at Harvard Law School is known for stress and rigor, for a few lawyer colleagues it represents a happy memory. The students used to meet and escape from cramming and legal drafting by watching Humphrey Bogart films. Many a long evening was passed with the actor's interpretation of memorable characters in films they saw over and over again. The 1941 film *The Maltese Falcon*, based on Dashiell Hammett's novel, was particularly unforgettable. When the lawyers needed to furnish their new offices in one of Manhattan's historic skyscrapers, they asked Bernt and Bill for assistance. The building dated from the 1920s—around the era of the novel—and so the designers decided to "team up" with the building and re-create the atmosphere of the partners' student years by designing everything to fit the set of *The Maltese Falcon*. All modern elements were removed, the ceiling was restored to its original height, the woodwork was darkened, and the wall-to-wall carpets were replaced by new wood floors with broad planks. Lamps, fittings, floors, door signs, paneling profiles, glass, and furniture: all might have been extracted from the film. When visitors enter the office the feeling is of walking into an interior that has remained unchanged since the 1930s or 1940s. Bogart himself might be leaning against a door frame saying "Of all the gin joints, in all the towns, in all the world, she walks into mine," just as he did in *Casablanca*. On a bookshelf stands a figure of a black falcon. Attorney names are sandblasted into the glass of the office doors, recalling the workplace of hard-baked detective Sam Spade. The ambience and the conviviality of the lawyers' student days are underscored and brought to life by the fact that these professionals now move around a film-set interior they used to admire in black and white. These days it is the lawyers who have the leading roles.

KODAK 400TX
A STORY AS
AS HIS
BLAZING
AUTOMATICS!
THOMAS TILLING LIMITED
SEQUOIA MARINE CORPORATION
THE HALCYON COMPANY
COFLEXIP S.A.
BLACK'S LAW DICTIONARY
WEST
THE ENCYCLOPEDIA OF MILITARY MODELING
RISK HOLDINGS, INC.
HANDBOOK OF MERGERS, ACQUISITIONS AND BUYOUTS
HARVARD
11

Kaffebaren Kroghs is tucked away in the Folketeater passage in Oslo. The building was completed in 1935 and it has housed both Folketeateret and Den Norske Opera. Heiberg Cummings wanted to give the coffee bar an atmosphere and ambiance that suggested it had been here ever since the building was new. Here delicious cakes and coffee are served by efficient waiters. **Schiller's, a tapas restaurant,** occupies a tiny room with a tiled floor, four to five high marble tables along yellow walls, and a long, narrow table in the gallery. And that's it. There is a large outdoor service area in the passage, a pleasant place to sit and watch people. Schiller's is inspired by the 1920s and characterized by rustic quality in everything from napkins and tableware to chairs and other furniture. **Cantina Cortina is a small Italian oasis** with authentic Italian cuisine. And the atmosphere is genuinely Italian. It creates a modern impression, though with a mix of new and old features.

Cortina
Dagens Lunsj
Melkesjokolade Pannacotta
1 L Fløte
75 G Sukker
1 STK Vanilje
3 Blad Gelantine
125 G Melkesjokolade
PANNACOTTA
CHIPS
BÆR
CRUMBLE
SAUS
Enomatic
Tignanello 07
Amarone 05

Melkesjokolade Pannacotta
1 L Fløte
75 G Sukker
1 STK Vanilje
3 Blad Gelantine
125 G Melkesjokolade
PANNACOTTA
CHIPS
CRUMBLE

Lena Tingstrøm has a soft voice, sensitive hands, and a clear, warm look. Her gentle touch is evident as, slowly and carefully, she shakes fabric—silk, linen, velvet, or wool; gray-green, deep violet, eggshell, or clear blue—so that it billows out and folds itself over the end of a large worktable. From the ceiling hangs the cord to a Swedish steam iron; on a low table stands a sewing machine that is more than twenty years old; on the enormous felt-covered worktable lies a box of pins with extra-large heads in all the colors of the rainbow, brought to Oslo from the garment district in New York. Lena explains the materials in detail and shows how threads and structure can change according to light, heat, or method of rolling. And then she gives a great smile and talks enthusiastically about hand stitching, fabric remnants, specially made fringes, and discovering worn pieces of fabric and borders in recycling stores or in old shop storerooms.

Lena's studio is located in the Heiberg Cummings Design offices in Oslo. The cooperation between Bernt, Bill, and Swedish-born Lena dates back to 1997. After gaining an advanced certificate in dressmaking, she started to work as a costume seamstress at the opera and as a creator of haute couture ball gowns. In England, she studied curtain sewing, specializing in sewing interlined curtains. She has made traditional curtains for the Nordic Museum and Tyresø Slott. And now she gives bedspreads, cushions, and curtains the same gracious treatment they would get were they to appear in an opera or a museum display. Her involvement in creating and staging Heiberg Cummings interiors is critical, and easily recognizable. The collaboration between Lena and Heiberg Cummings takes her back and forth between New York and Oslo. In New York, Flink usually sits on her lap while she sews. "Once Bernt and I were on our way to a client in Oslo, and he got me to follow him into an expensive furrier," Lena relates. "There he was wild about a beret in dark mink that he was convinced I had to have. It was absolutely not something I would have chosen myself, but I bought it even so. It's always like that when you are surrounded by Bernt's enthusiasm. It makes you bolder."

Lena sews curtains, cushions, and bedspreads according to the designers' instructions, but she also sets her distinctive fingerprint on the chosen fabrics. In one home she added a fringe of colored glass beads to a cushion. She made a fine border for the edge of a sofa in a Manhattan apartment. When a client from Oslo wanted a delicate linen curtain, Lena shortened the curtain in such a way that it looked as if it had acquired several pleats. In a home on Long Island lies a bedspread of thin velvet with broad backstitching in checkerwork. On Martha's Vineyard, transparent blinds in an eighteenth-century style boast threads held up by specially made hand-blown glass rings. Lena continues to compose cushions—firm and narrow, or large and soft—for benches designed by Bernt and Bill. She also makes monochrome or striped sofa cushions for Heiberg Cummings–designed armchairs.

"Textiles are alive," Lena says. "They can grow and behave unexpectedly. The color changes. The materials have power and mobility." Each new roll of material comes to life when she unfurls it like a veil over the studio table. "Just leap in, Lena—and get it finished," Bernt says. And so she does, with her gentle hands and profound knowledge.

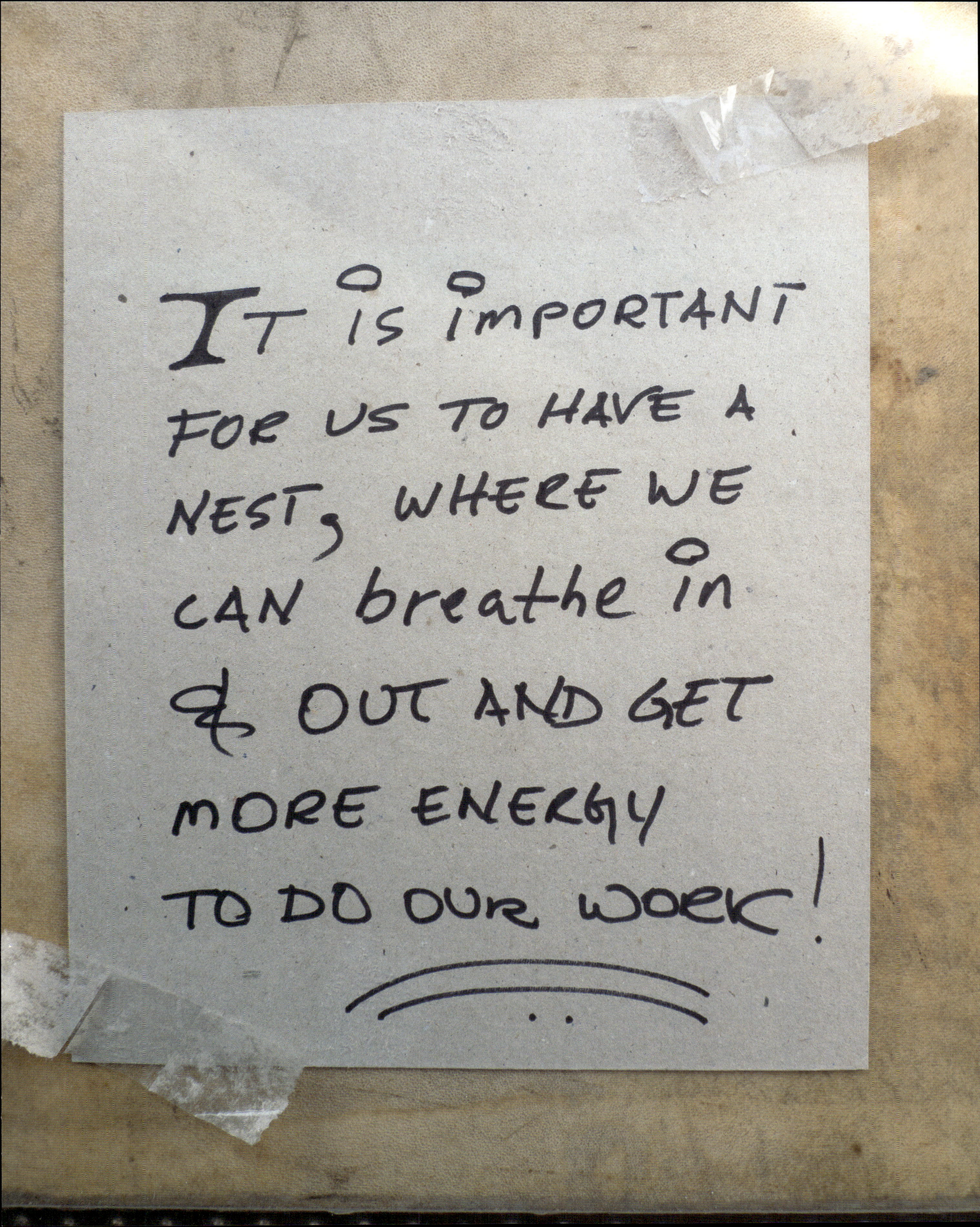
IT IS IMPORTANT
FOR US TO HAVE A
NEST, WHERE WE
CAN breathe in
& OUT AND GET
MORE ENERGY
TO DO OUR WORK!

BOMBAY
SAPPHIRE
Distilled
LONDON
DRY GIN
IMPORTED

Marcel Duchamp: How do you incorporate art into an interior. Is it function or ornament?

KODAK 400T
54
DAK 400TX
11

IMPERIAL

"Happiness is being married to your best friend." The house stands well back from a long, silver beach with breaking waves, in East Hampton on the east end of Long Island. Huge trees screen it from the sun. Magnolia, dogwood, and crabapple light up the neighborhood with their blossoms. In autumn, the leaves on the maple trees are a blaze of color. The owners had decided ideas about what they wanted their home to look like and how they wanted it to function. Their dream was to build a fantasy based on a traditional American farmhouse, to create a house that appeared to have always been there. Bernt and Bill's design looks as if it consists of an original core building to which sections have been added over the years. The architecture blends well with the style of the neighboring houses. From the road, the house looks discreet. The New England cottage–style facade has cedar shingle roofing, classical dormers in the gable of the steep-sloping roof, and a covered veranda where the owners can sit in high-backed rocking chairs and wave a welcome to visitors who come up the gravel path. The house is a solid structure designed for year-round use, and even though the summer is the best-known season for visiting the beach, it gives the impression of being a great place to celebrate Christmas and the New Year, when the snow insulates the walls and there is a howling gale outside.

MUNCH

KODAK
46
KODAK 400TX

HEIBERG CUMMINGS DESIGN
NYC-OSLO
HCD3
HEIBERG CUMMINGS
OSLO

Freedom and Plenty of Scope
Øivind Storm Bjerke and Svein Olav Hoff

Bill: When we begin to make an interior concept, it is vital that we understand the client—but also the location and its surroundings, the country we are operating in, and the local architecture we have to harmonize with.

Øivind: You have had clients you have worked for more than once. It is striking just how varied these projects can be. For one client you decorated an apartment in New York that is constructed around an art collection. For that same client you designed and furnished the interior of a summer house in a rural setting. The results differ so much that it is hard to believe that it is the same client and the same designers.

Bill: When people live in a town or a city, they like to lead an urban life, and they have definite ideas as to what that life should contain. When they go off into the country, they want to relax. Life acquires a completely different content, and this calls for a completely different concept. All people have different facets. They like to be different individuals—they feel this is exciting. They are the same, but their homes are extremely different—we use many of the same elements in both concepts, but they are not all that visible and manifest themselves physically in various ways.

Øivind: The aesthetic dimension is linked to the sensory experience of the physical properties of materials. You design cushions. You have them specially sewn. I can't help noticing that you are not only interested in patterns but also in choosing textiles on the basis of the tactile and thereby sensual qualities of the fabrics.

Bernt: It is the expression that determines things—whether we want a hard or a soft expression. We like to mix textures when it comes to fabrics but also when we do something like giving old French velour smoking chairs seats made of leather.

Bill: In that case, the client had to have the seat cushion replaced because the fabric was worn. In that way the history of the old chair was transferred to a completely new item of furniture.

Bernt: The choice of material is important. Leather that has been used and has aged over several years can become so beautiful. It acquires character. The same applies to fabrics—they gain a patina. We create furniture for various locations around the world. Bill is very much interested in the historical aspect when it comes to design. He likes to include certain historic elements, but with a modern twist. Bill has helped many people learn how to live with things. They can become worn; they can acquire a sheen. Many people are afraid of a scratch, a red-wine stain. It's very Norwegian for everything to have to be perfect. Instead, you have to learn to live with an interior—that gives it a lovely patina.

Bill: Yes, that's what I tell people. The first ring mark on a table is pure disaster. But when it's twenty years old, it starts to acquire a patina. As long as you operate with elements and materials that are genuine, they will start to live their own lives. And the interior just improves with age.

Bernt: That also applies to old craftsmanship. What used to happen if a plate got broken? It wasn't a catastrophe. It was neatly riveted with a small nail. And now that small plate means more to me than when it was perfect.

Bill: Somebody took care of it, you know.

Bernt: It acquires a history.

Bill: Exactly. I think it's interesting to talk about fashionable furnishings. When we work on an old house, we create a narrative that, with clashes and contrasts, is linked to the history the house has undergone.

Bernt: There is a particular house that I really love, that has many fine historic elements, that you can see has had a life. At one point in time, it was given large window surfaces that do not really belong. But I wouldn't dream of replacing them. They create the feeling of a house that has lived. It's often a pity when people over-renovate. Something of the history disappears at the same time.

Øivind: Modern architects often make a point of stressing the fracture between the old and the new.

Bernt: It can be wrong to make the break too obvious. Once we were working on a new kitchen for an old house in New Jersey. We chose to place the new kitchen in a completely new building at the rear of the old one. But to create a transition between the old and the new we found old planks in upstate New York that we could use for the floor. Other designers might have chosen a modern material, so that the kitchen would have a new look to it. In another project, a renovation of an oldish building, we had a fantastic client who shared our philosophical outlook. This was an assignment that took time. The local newspaper was also extremely interested in what was taking place. The work went on for a long time, for in actual fact the house was being almost completely rebuilt. From the outside, the renovation is virtually invisible, despite everything we have done. We simply made use of the old building elements. When everything was completed, the newspaper had a new article about the house that concluded that nothing had changed.

Bill: Our aim is for everything to become integrated into one narrative. An example from this project is the way we worked on the ceilings. In constructing the ceilings in the various parts of the building we introduced an alternation between new and old: we found old beams and then painted them. Painting them made them more discreet, and also helped to give the house a feeling of being old. At the same time, "the old" and "the new" harmonize in regard to colors and details, so that we get that perfect imperfection we have such a fondness for. It creates history but at the same time it is not a signal crying out for attention. The choice of materials can be used to give such small but important signals. In one location we inlaid a small leather edge in a banister—the soft against the hard. But visitors perhaps do not fully realize what it is that makes the experience of touching this banister so special. Perhaps they don't see it precisely because it is such a tiny detail. Don't shine the light on it. Make it an element that you discover later.

Svein Olav: Have you ever had clients suddenly contact you because they have seen the point of something you have done? Aha, they say, that's what it's all about!

Bill: Yes!

Svein Olav: When we talk about the past and the history leading up to today, do you feel you have reached your peak?

Bernt: I would not say we have reached our peak. There can be new summits. What gives us great freedom is our current situation. When you are fifty and you feel secure about what you are doing and where you are going, you have a greater scope for ideas. You have self-confidence, and that is when creating starts to be fun. That is when you are able to create something incredibly exciting.

Bill: It's also exciting to look back at our old projects. That's how we saw things then, we say, but we didn't really know that we thought like that. Today, we are better able to express and understand what we do.

Bernt: You can compare it to a visual artist who often protects his or her work until it is complete. We must likewise dare to say to our clients that we are the ones who are going to produce something that is the best for you.

Svein Olav: It's a fine attitude to life that you want to produce something that is the best for others. It's an attitude toward people that is truly marvelous.

STANDARD
№ 2
MAIL BOX

It is 10:28 in the morning in New Jersey. "I spend a lot of time folding curtains," a slight woman explains. With great precision, she smooths each section of the transparent wool curtains into three folds, stretching the material in straight lines and placing the end symmetrically and neatly on the dark floor. Order and structure appeal to the owner, who is a mathematician. It makes her feel that the home is secure and peaceful. Everything within is ordered in straight rows: in the cupboard and the refridgerator, items are arranged by size. In the wardrobe, clothes and shoes are sorted according to dimension and color. The sons' Lego blocks are laid out on a large board according to measurement and function. "Everything creates a structured framework for a hectic family life with four small children," she explains. "When we decided to polish up our 1896 house, it was a challenge to clear the various surfaces of distracting patterns and colors—we wanted to created ordered, well-dimensioned rooms. At the same time, we respected the history of the building and retained the original carvings and ornamentation. The kitchen is an addition, and Bill and Bernt helped me plan the dimensions on the basis of the measurements of the rectangular white tiles we had chosen for the walls, from floor to ceiling. We had specially made cupboards, doors, and windows, and we measured everything precisely, so that none of the tiles had to be divided."

The house from 1896 in a New York suburb has its original detailing, which retains its soul and history.

POSTE

NORTH SEA NEST

DESIGNERS BERNT HEIBERG AND BILL CUMMINGS BRING A NORDIC CHARM TO THEIR WEEKEND RETREAT IN SOUTHAMPTON

BY JORGE S. ARANGO | PHOTOGRAPHS BY ANASTASSIOS MENTIS

Sail Away | *On North Sea Harbor, the "beach shack" of Bernt Heiberg and Bill Cummings, of the New York design firm Heiberg Cummings, reflects their laid-back personalities and love of easy living. The designers spend a great deal of time enjoying the water at their back door. Cummings* (OPPOSITE) *pilots their 20-foot Chris Craft Speedster motorboat* (THIS PAGE), *which boasts a Norwegian flag—a nod to Heiberg's heritage. See Resources.*

A successful interior design project relies on a host of artisans, craftspeople, artists, designers, and architects. In this section we would like to thank all the people who have contributed in making each of these projects a success.

Pages 1 and 2
Notes from the sketchbook that Bill Cummings used in Warsaw, Poland, in 1990.

Pages 4–5
Introduction
Page 4 Self-portrait of Bernt Heiberg and Bill Cummings taken during the photography of the Summit, New Jersey, project, October 2010. Background: Contact sheet of photographs taken by Bill Cummings in Nantucket, Massachusetts, in 1988.

Pages 6–7
Childhood History
Clockwise from the top left: Bill Cummings on summer holiday with his family in Rome, 1967; Bill in Xenia, Ohio, in a production of Rogers & Hammerstein's musical *Oklahoma*; Ann and Bill Cummings Sr. in Amsterdam, 1967; Bernt Heiberg and Bill in Mykonos, Greece, 1998; Bernt's first day of school in Oslo, August 1968; Bernt painting Dee Kietan in New York, 1991.

Pages 8–11
Materials
Page 8 Eclectic mix of furnishings and objects from the first Heiberg Cummings Design studio in New York at 159 Madison Avenue. Page 11 Vignette of Bill and Bernt's first house in Oslo on Damstredet.

Pages 12–13
Article from *Elle Décor*, May 2003. Text by Mark Welsh, photography by William Waldron, produced by Elisabeth Sverbeyeff Byron.

Pages 14–35
Westport, Connecticut
Architect: Austin Patterson Disston Architects, LLC.
Interior design: Heiberg Cummings Design
Contractor: Tallman Building Co

Pages 14 and 17 Eighteenth-century Ivory tusks: Bijan Royal Inc. Page 19 Jaanika Peerna, Maelstrom Series, 2010, courtesy ARC Fine Art LLC; Light fixtures: Get Back Inc. Pages 20–23 Pendant lamps: Remains Antique Lighting. Page 24 Soft furnishings: Heiberg Cummings Design; Pendant lamps: Rejuvenation Hardware. Page 32-33 Chandelier: Bijan Royal Inc. Table top and candelabra: Bijan Royal Inc. Page 34 Club chair and sofa: Heiberg Cummings Design; Maria Noel, *Westbound*, 2010, courtesy ARC Fine Art LLC.

Pages 36–43
P. E. Guerin, Since 1857
Page 36 Knob archive. Page 37 Tie back selection. Page 38 Bernt Heiberg working with materials for a historic restoration in Oslo. Page 40 top left: Andrew F. Ward, current ownere of Guerin and Bernt Heiberg discussing details of the Oslo project; top center: Technician creating mould for custom hardware; top right: Ward discussing the importance discerning differences in qualities of materials; bottom left: Bernt reviewing historical references; bottom center: Technician fabricating mould; bottom right: Ward in New York factory. Page 41 top row: Drawings in the P. E. Guerin archive; second and third row: Heiberg and Ward supervising process in the factory; bottom right: comparing final result with original. Pages 42-43 Mould for custom faucet for the Oslo project.

Pages 44–55
Southampton, New York
Architect: Grosvenor Atterbury (1869–1956)
Renovation architect: Frank Greenwald Architect
Interior decoration: Heiberg Cummings Design
Window treatments: William Jelley
Landscape architecture: Joseph W. Tyree Landscape Design
Contractor: Wright & Company

Page 44 Ed Ruscha, *Parking Lots*, 1967/1999, thirty gelatin silver prints with mattes, archival artist's crate. Page 46 Richard Prince, *Untitled (Publicity)*, 1999; Richard Prince, *Untitled (Publicity)*, 2000. Page 46 Ottomans: Heiberg Cummings Design. Page 47 Richard Prince, *Untitled Fashion (Sunglasses, soda, and straw)*, 1982; Richard Prince, *Navy Nurse*, 2004; George Condo, *The Madman*, 2005; Dining table and chairs: B&B Italia; Round table: Armani Casa. Pages 48 and 49 David Hammons, *Close Your Eyes and See Black*, 1969; Alexander Calder, *Untitled*, Anish Kapoor, *Red Mirror*, 2008; George Condo, *The Madman*, 2005; George Condo, *Mother and Child*, 2010. Page 50 Keith Haring, *Untitled, September 26-27*;Table: Eighteenth-century Chinese table. Page 51 Edvard Munch, *Madonna*, 1895, included in the exhibition at Heiberg Cummings Studio, March 3, 2010, curated by Ina Johannesen; George Condo, *Untitled*. Page 51 Chair: Heiberg Cummings Design; Carpet: Ruby Beets. Pages 52 and 53 Catherine Opie, *Untitled (Surfers)* 2003; Richard Prince, *Upstate*, 1995–99; Richard Prince, *Runaway Nurse*, 2007. Page 54 Zhang Xiaogang, *Green Wall–About Sleep*, 2008, Sofa: Minotti. Page 55 Kitchen design and production: Eggersmann USA.

Pages 56–65
Semb Hovedgård, Horton, Norway
Interior architecture and design:
Heiberg Cummings Design
Window treatments and soft accessories:
Lena Tingstrom Drapery Design
Decorative painting: Robert Persson
Contractor: Jensen Byggteam

Pages 66–77
Vinderen, Oslo, Norway
Architect: Magnus Poulsson
Interior architecture and restoration:
Heiberg Cummings Design
Window treatments and pillows:
Lena Tingstrom Drapery Design

Pages 70 and 71 Mette Klaveness, *Untitled*. Page 73 Per Maning, *Untitled*. Pages 76 and 77 Original bathroom fixtures that were restored.

Pages 78–87
Nordmarka, Norway
Architect: Knut Støre & Anders Hokholt
Interior design: Heiberg Cummings Design
Window treatments and pillows:
Lena Tingstrom Drapery Design

Pages 78–79 Wood chopped by Harald Ramm.

Pages 88–101
Hardangervidda, Norway
Interior design: Heiberg Cummings Design
Architect: Harald Melbye
Window treatments, pillows, and covers:
Lena Tingstrom Drapery Design

Page 92 Soft furnishings: Heiberg Cummings Design. Page 94 Window treatment: Traditional Norwegian treatment fabricated by Lena Tingstrom Drapery Design. Page 95 Original painted finish on a nineteenth-century Norwegian framers chair. Page 97 Ruth Krefting, *Interior*, 1940s. Pages 98 and 99 Traditional Norwegian plate rack with Royal Copenhagen plates. Pages 100 and 101 Soft furnishings: Heiberg Cummings Design, Lighting: Refurbished traditional Norwegian fixtures.

Pages 102–109
Model house

Page 102 Model Silya Nymoen dressing in the window at the opening party for the new Heiberg Cummings Studio in the West Village, December 1, 2011. Page 105 Model house created in 1971 by Bernt Heiberg at age 10. Pages 106–107 Bill Cummings looking into the model house, March 2011. Pages 108–109 View through a window of the model house.

Pages 110–111
Exhibitions Heiberg Cummings Studios, 420 West 25th Street and 655 Washington Street, New York

Unni Askeland Paintings, October 30, 2008, organized by Turid Meeker Fine Art.
Knut Bry Photographs,September 16, 2009, organized by Turid Meeker Fine Art.
Thomas Pihl Paintings, November 12, 2009, organized by Turid Meeker FineArt.
Edvard Munch Works on Paper, March 3, 2010, organized by Ina Johannesen.
Cathrine Wessel Polaroid Photographs, December 1, 2011, organized by Turid Meeker Fine Art.

Page 110 Top right: Kunt Bry under his portrait of Grace Jones. Second row left: Ragnhild Gill, Tove Midelfart, Turid Meeker, and Madeleine Chapman at Thomas Pihl exhibition. Second row center: Bill Cummings and Bernt Heiberg with exhibition team at Edvard Munch exhibition. Second row right: George Soros at Edvard Munch exhibition. Third row left: Bernt Heiberg with guests at Edvard Munch exhibition. Third row middle: Unni Askeland at her exhibition. Third row right: Bill Cummings, Katie White, and Bernt Heiberg at Knut Bry exhibition. Fourth row left: Bill Cummings, Craig Meeker, Turid Meeker, Bernt Heiberg, Jan Vincents Johannessen, and Camilla Prytz at Thomas Pihl exhibition. Fourth row right: Carina Stolt-Nielsen Wikborg, Bill Cummings, Nicolas Stai, and Marika Kielland at Knut Bry exhibition.

Page 111 Catherine Wessel Exhibition Top row left: Bernt Heiberg, Bill Cummings and Flink in new West Village Studio; Top row right: Bernt Heiberg and Bill Cummings; Second row right and bottom row left: Silya Nymoen getting ready for her song; Bottom right: Katie White, Bernt Heiberg and Bill Cummings

Pages 112–23
Sørlandet, Norway
Interior Design: Heiberg Cummings Design
Architect: Lund Hagem Arkitekter
Contractor: Bico Bygg of Innredning

Page 116 Light fixtures, dining chairs and table: Ralph Pucci Gallery; Page 117 Patio furniture: David Sutherland. Page 119 Sofa: B&B ITALIA; Club chairs and table: Ralph Pucci Gallery; Ellen von Unwerth, *Bathing Beauties, Paris*, 1992, Courtesy Staley-Wise Gallery; Loose pillows: Lena Tingstrom Drapery Design.

Pages 124–35
Lamberts Cove, Martha's Vineyard Massachusetts
Interior design: Heiberg Cummings Design
Consulting architect: MacNelly Cohen Architects
Window treatment and pillows:
Lena Tingstrom Drapery Design
Window treatments and decorative accessories:
John Murphy by Tracker Home Décor
Contractors: Vineyard Construction Services Inc.,
Tate Builders Inc.
Local coordination: Sarah Doyle

Page 126 Kitchen design: Heiberg Cummings Design. Page 127 Wine cellar design: Heiberg Cummings Design. Page 129 Sofa: Heiberg Cummings Design; Reading lamps: Ralph Lauren. Page 130 Closet design: Heiberg Cummings Design. Page 131 Orkney chairs: Ralph Lauren; Coffee table with integrated cushions: Heiberg Cummings Design; Reading lamp: Objet Insolite Ltd. Page 132 Pillows: Heiberg Cummings Design; Powder room design: Heiberg Cummings Design; Hardware: Rocky Mountain Hardware, Bed: Atelier of Prague. Page 133 Daybed: Country Swedish; Chair and ottoman: Outdoor Design; Chaise longue (lower right): Heiberg Cummings Design; Reading lamp: Objet Inlolite Ltd. Page 134 Pendant light: Formations by Holly Hunt; Table: Nineteenth-century Irish farm table, Tracker Home Décor. Page 135 Pool furniture: Kingsley Bate.

Pages 136–43
Kristiansand, Norway
Architect: Knut Haaklau
Interior Design: Heiberg Cummings Design
Contractor: Bico Bygg of Innredning

Page 136–37 Dining chairs: Nancy Corzine. Page 138 Sofa: Knoll. Page 140 Wall shelf design: Heiberg Cummings Design. Pages 142 and 143 Chandelier: Holly Hunt; Dining chairs: Heiberg Cummings Design.

Pages 144–57
Tjøme, Norway
Architect: Jon Støre
Interior design: Heiberg Cummings Design
Window treatments, pillows and covers:
Lena Tingstrom Drapery Design
Contractor: Øyvind Tønnesen

Pages 146 and 147 Kitchen Design: Heiberg Cummings Design. Page 148 Blue plate: Maud Gjeruldsen Bugge; Pendant light fixture: Yoke Pendant by Studio by Visual Comfort. Page 149 Lars Jorde, *Sjøutsikt fra Hvasser*, 1920. Page 150 Charlotte Bergesen, *Ubåt*, 2003. Page 152 Marian Gromada, *Morgenstund*, 2005. Page 154 Top: Unknown artist, *skutemaleri* from the end of the nineteenth century; Unknown artist, *Blomster*, 1930s; Sofa: Heiberg Cummings Design; Coffee table: Formations by Holly Hunt. Bottom left: Kari Christiansen, *Fra Filtvet*, 1998. Sofa: Heiberg Cummings Design. Bottom center Lars Jorde, *Sjøutsikt fra Hvasser*, 1920. Bottom right : Sofa: Heiberg Cummings Design; Kristiania Chairs. Page 156 Unknown artist, *skutemaleri* from the end of the nineteenth century.

Page 158
Photograph by Kjersti Sundt Sissener.

Pages 160–61
Lake Tashmoo, Martha's Vineyard, Massachusetts
Interior architecture: Heiberg Cummings Design
Landscape architecture:
Horiuchi Solien Landscape Architecture
Architect: Hutker Architects
Contractor: Vineyard Construction Services Inc
Window treatments, pillows, and covers:
Lena Tingstrom Drapery Design
Decorative accessories: Tracker Home Decor

Page 163 Top right: Sofa: Heiberg Cummings Design; Floor lamp: Lorin Marsh Ltd.; Mirror and sconces: Eighteenth-century Swedish; Bottom right: Benches: Nineteenth-century Swedish purchased in Stockholm. Page 164 The house after demolition and ready for new construction. Page 165 Entrance and living room after renovations. The only original element is the fireplace. Chandelier: Holly Hunt. Page 167 Headboards: Heiberg Cummings Design; Wall lamps: Early twentieth-century Swedish.

Pages 168–73
Sagaponack, New York
Interior design and furnishings:
Heiberg Cummings Design
Draperies and pillows: William Jelley

Page 170 Yoke pendant light fixture: Studio by Visual Comfort; Table: Charles Pollack by William Switzer; Chairs: Charles Fradin by John Rosselli. Page 171 Stone bench: Formations by Holly Hunt; Bed and sofa: Heiberg Cummings Design; Bedside lamp: Visual Comfort; Ross Bleckner, *Yellow Rose*. Page 172 Console table: Gregorious Pineo; Upholstered bench: Maxine Snider; Sofa: Dennis & Leen by Holly Hunt; Coffee table: Formations by Holly Hunt; Club chair: Heiberg Cummings Design; Console table behind sofa: Carole Gratale Inc. Page 173 Commode: Holly Hunt; Lamp: Visual Comfort

Pages 174–77
Sarasota, Florida
Architect: Clifford M. Scholz Architects, LLC
Interior Design: Heiberg Cummings Design
Contractor: MI Collingwood General Contractor

Pages 176 and 177 Furniture: Formations by Holly Hunt.

Pages 180–85
Central Park West, Manhattan
Interior design: Heiberg Cummings Design
Architect: Robert A. M. Stern Architects
Contractor: Perfect Home Improvement
Window treatments and pillows: William Jelley
Art installation: Turid Meeker Contemporary Art

Page 182 Black lacquer commode: High Style Deco; Norman Bluhm, *Untitled*, c. 1960, courtesy Loretta Howard Gallery, sourced and supplied by Turid Meeker Contemporary Art. Page 183 Side table (lower left): Studio h by Holly Hunt; Club chair and ottoman: Mattallano by Holly Hunt; Olav Christopher Jenssen, *The Bretagne No.9, Berlin 2010*, courtesy the artist and Tracy Williams Ltd., sourced and supplied by Turid Meeker Contemporary Art. Page 183 Bottom photograph: Console table: Lyle & Umbach by Holly Hunt, Mirror: Ron Seff, Chandelier: High Style Deco, Dining table and chairs: J. Robert Scott. Page 184 Ottoman: Michele Bonan by Chelini S.P.A., Coffee table: J. Robert Scott. Page 185 Club chair: Studio h by Holly Hunt, Side table: High Style Deco.

Pages 186–89
Pied-à-terre, Manhattan
Interior Design and Architecture:
Heiberg Cummings Design
Contractor: Perfect Home Improvement, Inc.

Page 188 Cornelia Parker, *Alter Ego*, 2010 (Cold Water) silver plated objects - 2 units one intact one squashed 250 ton industrial press. Boyd Webb, *Bedding II*, 1983/2006, courtesy Boyd Webb and Sonnabend Gallery, sourced by Turid Meeker Contemporary Art; Gene Davis, *Blue Cloud*, courtesy Loretta Howard Gallery. Page 189 Terry Winters, *Indigo Sequence / 5*, 2004, courtesy the artist and Matthew Marks Gallery, sourced by Turid Meeker Contemporary Art; Heather Rowe, *The Third Window*, 2010.

Pages 190 – 193
Gyldenløvesgate, Oslo Norway

Page 193 Kjell Erik Killi Olsen, *Untitled*.

Pages 194 – 201
Upper East Side, Manhattan
Interior architecture: Heiberg Cummings Design
Contractor: Creative Structures Inc. and
Perfect Home Improvement Inc.
Window treatments and pillows: William Jelley

Page 194 Headboard and frame: Roger Arlington. Page 196 Games table: Dessin fournir by Holly Hunt; Sofa: Christian Liaigre by Holly Hunt, Spiral occasional table: Hinson & Company. Page 197 Candle shade: Armani Casa, Mirror: High Style Deco. Page 200 Dressing table and lamps: High Style Deco.

Pages 202–213
Soho, Manhattan
Interior Architecture and Design:
Heiberg Cummings Design
Consulting Architect: ADG Architecture and Design
Window treatments, pillows and covers:
Lena Tingstrom Drapery Design
Contractor: Silverlinning Interiors
Art installation: Turid Meeker Contemporary Art

Page 202 Helmut Newton, *Jenny Capitain in My Studio, Paris* 1978, courtesy Staley-Wise Gallery; Helmut Newton, *Big Nude I, Paris*, 1979, courtesy Staley-Wise Gallery; Chair: Heiberg Cummings Design.

Page 204 Herb Ritts, *Alec Wek, Los Angeles*, 1995, courtesy Staley-Wise Gallery; Robert Mapplethorpe, *Ken and Lydia and Tyler*, 1985, © Robert Mapplethorpe Foundation, courtesy Sean Kelly Gallery; Robert Mapplethorpe, *Irises*, 1986, © Robert Mapplethorpe Foundation, courtesy Sean Kelly Gallery; Herb Ritts, *Djimon, Three-Quarter Nude, Profile, Hollywood*, 1989, courtesy Fahey/Klein Gallery; Herb Ritts, *Djimon, frontal View, Hollywood*, 1989, courtesy Staley-Wise Gallery. Sofa: Ralph Lauren. Bentwood and leather chair: Heiberg Cummings Design.

Page 205 Robert Mapplethorpe, *Lisa Lyon*, (unique construction),1981, © Robert Mapplethorpe Foundation, courtesy Sean Kelly Gallery; Robert Mapplethorpe, *Mark Stevens*, (Mr. 10 1/2),1976, © Robert Mapplethorpe Foundation, courtesy Sean Kelly Gallery; Andre Kertesz, *Melancholic Tulip, NY*, 1939, courtesy Staley-Wise Gallery.

Page 206 Kitchen design: Heiberg Cummings Design; Kitchen production: Ted Bravakis Toronto. Tall table: Heiberg Cummings Design. Page 207 Peter Lindbergh, *Mathilde on Eiffel Tower (Homage to Erwin Blumenfeld and Marc Riboud), Rolling Stones, Paris*, 1989, courtesy Kennedy Boesky Photographs; Len Prince, *Arm and Torso, Nigel, New York City*, 1990, courtesy Staley-Wise Gallery; Herb Ritts, *Cindy Crawford, Costa Carees*, 1998, courtesy Staley-Wise Gallery; Herb Ritts, *Fred with Tires, Hollywood*, 1984, courtesy Staley-Wise Gallery; Herb Ritts, *Male Torso with Veil (tight), Silverlake*, 1985, courtesy Staley-Wise Gallery; Robert Mapplethorpe, *Thomas*, 1987, © Robert Mapplethorpe Foundation, courtesy Sean Kelly Gallery; Bruce Weber, *Camp Pot Luck, Spitfire Lake*, 1999, courtesy the artist and Robert Miller Gallery; Herb Ritts, *Waterfall II, Hollywood*, 1988, courtesy Fahey/Klein Gallery; Peter Lindbergh, *Lynn Koester-Pin-Up, Studio, Paris*, 1986, courtesy Kennedy Boesky Photographs; Bruce Weber, *Islamorada, Florida*, 1999, courtesy the artist and Robert Miller Gallery; Horst P. Horst, *Round the Clock*, 1987, courtesy Kennedy Boesky Photographs; Helmut Newton, *Elsa Peretti, New York*. 1975, courtesy Staley-Wise Gallery; Ross Bleckner, *Untitled*, 1981, courtesy the artist and Kagan Martos Gallery.

Page 208 Robert Mapplethorpe, *Tulip*, 1988, © Robert Mapplethorpe Foundation, courtesy Sean Kelly Gallery.

Page 209 Robert Mapplethorpe, *Apollo*, 1988, © Robert Mapplethorpe Foundation, courtesy Sean Kelly Gallery; Pendant fixture: Kevin Reilly by Holly Hunt; Dining table: Studio h by Holly Hunt, Dining chairs: Heiberg Cummings Design.

Pages 210 and 211 Horst P. Horst, *Male Nude (legs crossed)*, 1952, courtesy Staley-Wise Gallery; Horst P. Horst, *Back Study*, 1952, courtesy Staley-Wise Gallery. Horst P. Horst, *Prostrate Male Nude*, 1952, courtesy Galerie Volker Diehl; Robert Mapplethorpe, *Doris Saatchi*, 1983, © Robert Mapplethorpe Foundation, courtesy Sean Kelly Gallery; Robert Mapplethorpe, *Self-Portrait*, 1980, © Robert Mapplethorpe Foundation, courtesy Sean Kelly Gallery; Sofas: Heiberg Cummings Design; Coffee table: Holly Hunt; Occasional tables: Pierce Martin.

Page 212 Helmut Newton, *Nude Descending Stairs, Nice*, 1981, courtesy Staley-Wise Gallery; Helmut Newton, *Jodi Foster, Hollywood*, 1987, courtesy Staley-Wise Gallery, Helmut Newton, *Veruschka in Nice*, 1975, courtesy Staley-Wise Gallery; Helmut Newton, *Lisa Lyon*, 1980, courtesy Staley-Wise Gallery; Helmut Newton, *Patti Hansen Over Manhattan*, 1977, courtesy Staley-Wise Gallery; Helmut Newton, *Natasha Kinski, Hollywood*, 1983, courtesy Staley-Wise Gallery; Helmut Newton, *In My Studio, Paris*, 1978, courtesy Staley-Wise Gallery; Helmut Newton, *Sylvia in My Studio at Night, Paris*, 1981, courtesy Staley-Wise Gallery; Helmut Newton, *Arielle IX (from Arielle)*, 1982, courtesy Staley-Wise Gallery; Headboards: Heiberg Cummings Design.

Page 213 Robert Mapplethorpe, *Tulips*, 1986, © Robert Mapplethorpe Foundation, courtesy Sean Kelly Gallery; Len Prince, *Olympian Puerto Rico Swimmer*, 1992, courtesy Staley-Wise Gallery; Herb Ritts, *Carrie in Sand, Paradise Cove*, 1988, courtesy Fahey/Klein Gallery.

Pages 214–215
Launch of Hødnebø collection at Gamle Logen in Oslo, August 30, 2007. Photograph by Jim Hinsley. Performance created and directed by Anna Gutto and Ane Skumsvoll.

Pages 216–219
Heiberg Cummings Installation at Kaare Berntsen Gallery, August 25, 2010
"People are part of an interior environment"
Photographs by Fabian Greenberg
Performance production: Tiril Pharo and Anna Gutto

Page 216 Bendik Østbye Johannessen and Tiril Pharo dining interpretation. Page 218 Bottom left: Jarl Flaaten Bjørk and Ulla Broch performing a dining interpretation. Bottom right: Siv Endresen with husband Christian. Far right: Bernt's mother Elisabeth Heiberg Svendby with cousin Wenche Heiberg. Page 219: Top center: Harald Wold Reitan entering event with Else Ramm and Ole Edvard Reitan. Top right: Bendik Østbye Johannessen and Tiril Pharo greeting guests. Second row left: Jarl Flaaten Bjørk and Silya Nymoen with guests. Third row left: Kaare Berntsen with guests. Jarl Flaaten Bjørk in background. Bottom left: Bernt greeting guests. Bottom right: Ulla Broch installed in exhibition.

Pages 220–21
Bernt Heiberg Birthday
N.A.L.L. Foundation, Vence, France
June 13, 2011

Pages 222– 237
Poiesis

Page 222 Self-portrait from Ivar Aasensvei in Oslo, August 2011. Page 224 Books in house on North Sea Harbor, Southampton. Page 226 Self-portrait taken in Robert Wilson's bathroom at Watermill Foundation. Page 231 Ane Skumsvoll at the launch of Hødnebø collection at Gamle Logen in Oslo, August 30, 2007. Photograph by Jim Hinsley. Performance created and directed by Anna Gutto and Ane Skumsvoll. Page 232 Anna Gutto sitting in a conceptual interior created to illustrate how the client's inner passions are integrated into an interior. Page 234 Ceiling in guest bedroom at Bluewater Lane, Westport, Connecticut. Page 237 Furniture collection launch for Hødnebø, August 30, 2007. Interest and intrigue added by Øystein Haugerud in the Gamle Logen in Oslo. Photograph by Jim Hensely. Performance created and directed by Anna Gutto and Ane Skumsvoll.

Pages 238–243
Stairs Dillenbeck Finley Law Offices,
Union Square, New York
Architecture and Interior Design: Heiberg Cummings Design
Contractor: Remodella Corp.

Page 238 Stanley T. Stairs and John J. Finley in their newly renovated offices. Model in background: Silya Nymoen. Page 239 Reception area. Tall table: Heiberg Cummings Design. Page 240 Finley's office, which incorporates his love of classic movies and his own furnishings. Page 241 top left: Meeting room with prints by Robert Wilson. Top right: Stairs in his office. Bottom: Stairs and model Silya Nymoen. Pages 242 and 243 Artifacts and memorabilia from the movie *The Maltese Falcon*.

Pages 244–49
Folketeaterpassasjen, Oslo, Norway
Schillers Tapas
Cantina Cortina
Christian Krogh cafe
Interior architecture and design:
Heiberg Cummings Design
Project coordinator: Siv Endresen

Page 244 Cantina Cortina
Page 245 Christian Krogh Cafe

Page 246 Schillers Tapas
Page 247 Cantina Cortina
Page 248 Entrance to Cantina Cortina
Page 249 Interior details, Christian Krogh Café

PAGES 250–51
LENA TINGSTROM

Page 251 Lena Tingstrom at work in Heiberg Cummings Oslo studio on Magnus Berg Gate and Gimleveien, Oslo

PAGES 252–257
NORTH SEA HARBOR, SOUTHAMPTON, NEW YORK
Summer home of Bernt Heiberg and Bill Cummings
Window treatments: New York Shutter Company
Pillows and covers: Lena Tinstrom Drapery Design

Page 254 Pendant lamp: Visual Comfort; Sofa: Heiberg Cummings Design; Bench/coffee table: Heiberg Cummings Design. Page 255 Kitchen island: Whispers & Breezes Antiques; Track lighting: Times Square Lighting. Page 256 Vanity and sink: Kohler. Page 257 Dining table and benches: Heiberg Cummings Design. Page 255 Top left: A summer party, from left: Eve Faye, Abby Terkuhle, Jeff Sherwood, Donna Parker, Pauline, Julio Hernandez, Stacy Cohen, Paul Davis, Carole Rochas, Jeanette Kvisvik, Roland Nivelais, and Bernt Heiberg.

PAGES 258–59
BILL CUMMINGS BIRTHDAY
NORTH SEA HARBOR, SOUTHAMPTON, NEW YORK
JULY 18, 2010

PAGES 260–65
SAGG ROAD, SAGAPONACK, NEW YORK
Interior Design: Heiberg Cummings Design
Draperies, loose pillows, covers, and headboards:
Lena Tingstrom Drapery Design

Page 264 Tall table, plate racks, dining table: Heiberg Cummings Design; Sono Oasto, *Small Wire Drawings*, 2003. Cup holder: not by Marcel Duchamp. Page 265 Soft furnishings: Heiberg Cummings Design

PAGES 266–73
EAST HAMPTON, NEW YORK
Architectural design: Heiberg Cummings Design
Consulting architect: Shawn F. Leonard Architect, AIA
Contractor: Sandpebble Builders, Inc.
Interior design: Heiberg Cummings Design
Landscape architecture:
Horiuchi Solien Landscape Architecture
Draperies, pillows and covers:
Lena Tinstrom Drapery Design
Light fixtures: Suffolk Designer
Lighting, Inc. by Visual Comfort

Page 268 Soft furniture: Heiberg Cummings Design.

PAGES 274–77
HEIBERG CUMMINGS, GREENWICH VILLAGE STUDIO,
655 WASHINGTON STREET, NEW YORK

Page 274 Bill and Bernt in front of their new studio, December 2011. Photograph by Carl Erik Hagen. Page 277 Fabric sample filing system.

PAGES 278–291
SUMMIT, NEW JERSEY
Interior Design: Heiberg Cummings Design
Window treatments and pillows:
Lena Tingstrom Drapery Design

Pages 282–83 Sofas and ottoman: Lucca. Page 284 Sofa: Roger Arlington, Club chairs: Dessin fournir by Holly Hunt, Coffee tables: Nancy Corzine, Bench under window: Christian Liaigre by Holly Hunt. Page 285 Ottomans: Christian Liaigre by Holly Hunt. Page 289 Anne Katrine Senstad, *Light on Wall*; Dining table: Christian Liaigre by Holly Hunt. Pendant light: Philippe Starck, Dining chairs: Christian Liaigre by Holly Hunt. Pages 290–91 Kitchen production: Ted Bravakis Toronto.

PAGES 292–99
NORTH HAVEN, NEW YORK
Architecture and interior design: Heiberg Cummings Design
Contractor: Dan Loos Construction

Pages 292–93 Wall lights on terrace: Tekna by Circa Antique. Page 294 Kitchen Design: Heiberg Cummings Design; Kitchen basket, living room pendant lights: Kari Struss, Lauren Copen Antiques; Vanity: Heiberg Cummings Design. Page 298 Door and closet design: Heiberg Cummings Design. Page 299 Wall lamps: Ralph Lauren by Visual Comfort.

PAGES 300–301
Article from *Hamptons Cottages and Gardens*, August 1–15 2007, written by Jorge S. Arango with photographs by Anastassios Mentis.

Published in the United States by The Monacelli Press LLC

Library of Congress Control Number: 2012940146
ISBN 978-158093-347-6

Design: Gina Rose Design
English edition typography: Susan Evans, Design per se

Printed in Poland

U.S.
COLOR LABS
KODAK 400TX
46